Study Guide for Decoding Julius Caesar

With Typical Questions and Answers

Steven Smith

Sherwood Press

CONTENTS

— • —

How to use this guide

This analysis of William Shakespeare's "Julius Caesar" intends to offer a study guide to readers who need a more in-depth view of the story.

This book is divided into questions, so the answers appear in a short essay style and may include repeated information. The questions are typical of what a high school student may experience.

I want to think all important questions have been either directly or indirectly answered. However, if you, the reader, feel something is missing, please reach out to me, and I will add it!

Happy studying!
Steven Smith
stevensmithvo@gmail.com
www.classicbooksexplained.com

— · —

Historical background to William Shakespeare

William Shakespeare, often regarded as the greatest writer in the English language and the world's pre-eminent dramatist, was born in 1564 in Stratford-upon-Avon, England. The exact date of his birth is not known, but it is traditionally observed on April 23, Saint George's Day.

Shakespeare's father, John Shakespeare, was a glove-maker and a local political figure. His mother, Mary Arden, was the daughter of a prosperous landowning farmer. Shakespeare had two older sisters and three younger brothers.

He likely attended the King's New School, a free chartered grammar school in Stratford, where he would have studied rhetoric, grammar, and classics. It was here that he first encountered Latin drama and literature, which had a significant influence on his later works.

At the age of 18, he married Anne Hathaway, a woman eight years his senior. They had three children: Susanna, and twins Hamnet and Judith. Sadly, Hamnet died at the age of 11, an event that is thought to have deeply affected Shakespeare.

In the late 1580s, Shakespeare arrived in London and began his career as an actor and a playwright. By 1592, he had achieved success in both roles, with his plays being produced and performed by several companies.

In 1594, he became a founding member of the Lord Chamberlain's Men, a company of actors. The company was very successful, later becoming the King's Men in 1603 when King James I ascended the throne and became the company's patron. The troupe owned the Globe Theatre and the Blackfriars Theatre, and they produced most of Shakespeare's plays.

Over his 20-year career, Shakespeare wrote about 39 plays, 154 sonnets, and two long narrative poems. His plays cover a range of genres, including histories, tragedies, comedies, and tragicomedies (romances).

Shakespeare retired from public life around 1613 and returned to Stratford-upon-Avon, where he died on April 23, 1616 at the age of 52. Despite his relatively short life, his prolific output and profound influence on literature, drama, and culture have made him one of the most enduring figures in literary history.

—·—

HISTORICAL BACKGROUND TO JULIUS CAESAR

"Julius Caesar" is one of William Shakespeare's historical tragedies, composed around 1599. While Shakespeare's plays often take creative liberties with historical facts, "Julius Caesar" is based on real events in Roman history, most notably the assassination of Julius Caesar in 44 BC and the subsequent power struggles in Rome.

Historically, Julius Caesar was a prominent military general who had won a number of significant victories for Rome, especially in Gaul. Over time, he amassed substantial political power, to the point where he declared himself 'dictator perpetuo', or dictator in perpetuity. This move deeply concerned several Roman senators who believed that Caesar aimed to overthrow the Republic and establish a monarchy. These senators, including Brutus, Cassius, and others, formed a conspiracy and assassinated Caesar in the Senate on the Ides of March (March 15), 44 BC.

Following Caesar's assassination, Rome was thrown into chaos. Caesar's ally and friend, Mark Antony, leveraged the situation to turn the public opinion against the conspirators, leading to civil war. Eventually, Octavian (later known as Augustus), Caesar's adopted heir, defeated all rivals and established himself as the first Roman Emperor, signaling the end of the Roman Republic and the beginning of the Roman Empire.

Shakespeare's "Julius Caesar" takes these historical events and adds layers of human drama, philosophical introspection, and political intrigue. He drew much of his information from Plutarch's "Lives", a series of biographies of famous Greeks and Romans, including Caesar, Brutus, and Antony. Plutarch's "Lives" was translated into English by Sir Thomas North in 1579, providing Shakespeare with a historical and narrative resource for his play. Shakespeare made good use of this source, but, as always, added his own dramatic flair and thematic depth.

While "Julius Caesar" has a historical backdrop, it's important to understand that Shakespeare uses history as a stage for exploring universal human themes such as friendship, honor, ambition, and the power of rhetoric. Therefore, while it provides insight into a key moment in Roman history, the play is not strictly a historical account but rather a timeless exploration of political and personal conflict.

— · —

WHY DO STUDENTS STUDY JULIUS CAESAR

Studying William Shakespeare's "Julius Caesar" offers students a multitude of benefits across a range of academic and personal skills:

1. **Understanding of historical events**: While "Julius Caesar" is not a strict historical account, it does provide insight into significant events in Roman history, such as Caesar's assassination and its aftermath. This helps students gain a sense of the political and social dynamics of the time.

2. **Literary appreciation**: Shakespeare's works are celebrated for their compelling storytelling, profound themes, and linguistic artistry. "Julius Caesar" is a powerful example of Shakespeare's skill in character development and dramatic structure.

3. **Language and vocabulary skills**: Shakespeare's plays are renowned for their rich language and inventive use of words and phrases. Studying "Julius Caesar" can expand students' vocabulary and help them appreciate the flexibility and expressive potential of the English language.

4. **Critical thinking and analytical skills**: The play delves into complex themes like power, loyalty, ambition, and manipulation. Analyzing these themes encourages students to think critically about the characters' motivations and actions, the consequences of those actions, and the broader implications for society.

5. **Understanding of rhetorical devices**: "Julius Caesar" is notable for its use of persuasive rhetoric, particularly in Antony's famous "Friends, Romans, countrymen" speech. Studying these speeches can enhance students' understanding of rhetoric and its power to influence and manipulate.

6. **Cultural literacy**: Given the global recognition and influence of Shakespeare's works, studying "Julius Caesar" contributes to cultural literacy. Many phrases from the play have entered common usage (e.g., "Beware the Ides of March," "Et tu, Brute?"), and recognizing these references can enrich students' understanding of other texts and cultural products.

7. **Empathy and human understanding**: As with all literature, "Julius Caesar" offers insights into human nature and behavior. It encourages students to empathize with different characters and understand their perspectives, thereby fostering emotional intelligence and human understanding.

8. **Political Philosophy and Ethical Dilemmas**: "Julius Caesar" delves into complex political themes, exploring questions about leadership, power, and the morality of political assassination. Students can engage with these ideas, fostering a deeper understanding of political philosophy and ethics.

9. **Public Speaking and Performance Skills**: Studying plays like "Julius Caesar" provides students with the opportunity to read, recite, or perform dramatic scenes, which can help improve public speaking and performance skills.

10. **Understanding of Dramatic Devices**: As a playwright, Shakespeare employed various dramatic techniques, including fore-

shadowing, dramatic irony, soliloquies, and asides. By studying "Julius Caesar", students can learn about these devices and how they contribute to the development of plot and character.

11. **Cultural and Historical Context**: Studying "Julius Caesar" offers insight into the Elizabethan era's cultural and historical context, when the play was written. This can provide a deeper understanding of the play and foster a broader knowledge of world history.

12. **Comparative Literature**: Shakespeare's play can be compared and contrasted with other literary works, whether they be other plays by Shakespeare, classical works of tragedy, or modern narratives. This can help students appreciate the breadth and depth of literature.

13. **Creativity**: Finally, studying "Julius Caesar" can inspire creativity. Students might be motivated to write or perform their own versions of scenes, or to imagine alternative outcomes or character interpretations.

In short, studying "Julius Caesar", like other works of Shakespeare, provides an interdisciplinary learning experience that bridges literature, history, philosophy, and the performing arts.

— • —

NEW LANGUAGE AND VOCABULARY SKILLS

When studying Shakespeare's "Julius Caesar," students learn a variety of language skills and encounter a broad range of vocabulary, some of which are specific to the period in which the play was written. The dialogue in "Julius Caesar" presents a number of linguistic features and literary devices that can enrich students' understanding of English.

1. **Elizabethan Vocabulary**: Shakespeare's plays introduce students to numerous words and phrases that were common in the Elizabethan era but are less familiar to modern readers. For example, the term "hie" (Act 1, Scene 3) means to hurry or hasten, and "knave" (Act 1, Scene 2) is a term for a deceitful man or rascal.

2. **Archaic Language**: Shakespeare's language often uses grammatical structures and verb forms that are no longer common in modern English. This includes the use of "thou," "thee," "thy," and "thine" for "you" and "your," and verbs that end in "-est" or "-eth" for second and third-person singular present tense, like "thou sayest" (you say) or "he doth" (he does). For instance, in Act 2, Scene 1, Brutus uses the phrase "thou sleep'st" (you sleep).

3. **New Vocabulary**: Shakespeare's works are known for their extensive vocabulary. Reading his plays can introduce readers to a variety of new words, many of which are still used in modern English. For example, words such as "beseech" (to beg), "valiant"

(brave), or "prodigious" (enormous) can expand a student's language use.

4. **Understanding References**: Many phrases from Shakespeare's plays have entered the English language and are frequently used in literature, media, and everyday conversation. Recognizing these phrases, such as "Beware the Ides of March" or "Et tu, Brute?", can enhance a student's cultural and linguistic understanding.

5. **Figurative Language**: "Julius Caesar" includes numerous examples of figurative language, such as metaphors and similes, which can expand students' understanding of how language can convey complex ideas and emotions. For example, Cassius uses a metaphor in Act 1, Scene 2 when he says, "The fault, dear Brutus, is not in our stars / But in ourselves, that we are underlings."

6. **Wordplay and Puns**: Shakespeare frequently uses puns and other forms of wordplay, which can sharpen students' attention to the multiple meanings of words. For instance, in Act 1, Scene 2, a cobbler describes himself as a "mender of bad soles," a pun on "souls."

7. **Idiomatic Expressions**: Shakespeare's plays have given us many idiomatic expressions that are still widely used today. For example, the warning "Beware the Ides of March" from Act 1, Scene 2 is often used to signify an impending disaster.

8. **Poetry and Rhythm**: Shakespeare often writes in iambic pentameter, a poetic meter that can enhance students' appreciation for rhythm and musicality in language. An example of iambic pentameter from Act 1, Scene 2 is "I know that virtue to be in you, Brutus."

By studying these linguistic elements in "Julius Caesar," students can gain a deeper understanding of English language structures, expand their vocabulary, and develop an appreciation for the richness and versatility of language.

Describe the character development

In Shakespeare's "Julius Caesar", there is significant character development, especially for Brutus, Cassius, Julius Caesar, and Mark Antony. The characters change and grow through their actions, decisions, and interactions with others.

1. **Brutus**: At the beginning of the play, Brutus is portrayed as a respected Roman senator who is close to Caesar but is also highly concerned about the republic. He is torn between his loyalty to Caesar and his political ideals. When Cassius manipulates him into believing that Caesar's ambition will end the republic, Brutus, with a heavy heart, joins the conspiracy against Caesar. This decision shows his development from a passive character into an active participant in the political game. By the end of the play, he recognizes the tragic error of his decision to assassinate Caesar (Act 5, Scene 5, "O Julius Caesar, thou art mighty yet! Thy spirit walks abroad, and turns our swords in our own proper entrails.") This shows Brutus's ultimate development from a patriot to a tragic hero.

2. **Cassius**: Cassius is one of the main conspirators against Caesar and is the one who recruits Brutus into the plot. He is initially presented as a manipulative character driven by envy and ambition. As the play progresses, however, he shows genuine concern for Brutus and even concedes to Brutus's strategic decisions despite

his own better judgement, indicating a shift from self-interest to loyalty and friendship (Act 4, Scene 3, "Then, with your will, go on; we'll along ourselves, and meet them at Philippi.")

3. **Julius Caesar**: Caesar is depicted as a powerful, superstitious, and perhaps arrogant figure. Despite multiple warnings about his impending death (like the Soothsayer's "Beware the Ides of March" in Act 1, Scene 2, and Calpurnia's prophetic dream in Act 2, Scene 2), he attends the Senate and is assassinated. His dismissal of the warnings shows an overconfidence that develops from his initial depiction as a capable leader to an arguably arrogant man ignoring dangers.

4. **Mark Antony**: Antony begins as a loyal friend to Caesar and seems less politically ambitious. However, after Caesar's assassination, he delivers one of the most famous speeches in literature ("Friends, Romans, countrymen, lend me your ears; I come to bury Caesar, not to praise him." in Act 3, Scene 2). This speech incites the crowd against the conspirators, indicating a significant transformation in his character—from a seemingly frivolous loyalist to a shrewd and powerful orator and political strategist. By the end of the play, Antony has fully emerged as a force to be reckoned with, setting the stage for the ensuing power struggle in Rome.

These characters' development is a critical aspect of "Julius Caesar", adding depth and complexity to the narrative and themes of the play.

Examples of Understanding of Rhetorical Devices

Shakespeare's "Julius Caesar" is rich with rhetorical devices, which serve to make arguments more persuasive, moving, or eloquent. Here are some examples:

1. **Ethos**: Ethos is an appeal to the speaker's credibility or character. Brutus uses ethos in his speech to the citizens of Rome after the assassination, as he points to his reputation for honesty to make the people believe he killed Caesar for the good of Rome: "Believe me for mine honor, and have respect to mine honor..." (Act 3, Scene 2).

2. **Pathos**: Pathos is an appeal to emotions. Mark Antony effectively employs pathos in his speech, pulling at the citizens' heartstrings as he points out the wounds on Caesar's body and reminds them of Caesar's kindness and generosity: "Look, in this place ran Cassius' dagger through: See what a rent the envious Casca made: Through this the well-beloved Brutus stabb'd..." (Act 3, Scene 2).

3. **Logos**: Logos is an appeal to logic or reason. Brutus tries to use logos in his speech to the Romans, presenting the logical argument that they would have ended up as slaves if Caesar had lived: "Had you rather Caesar were living and die all slaves, than that Caesar were dead, to live all free men?" (Act 3, Scene 2).

4. **Rhetorical Questions**: Rhetorical questions are asked not to get an answer but to emphasize a point. Mark Antony uses this technique skillfully in his speech, asking questions to which the answer is clearly no, thereby making the crowd question Brutus's claim that Caesar was ambitious: "You all did see that on the Lupercal I thrice presented him a kingly crown, which he did thrice refuse: was this ambition?" (Act 3, Scene 2).

5. **Antithesis**: Antithesis is the juxtaposition of contrasting ideas. Mark Antony uses antithesis when he says, "But here's a parchment with the seal of Caesar; I found it in his closet, 'tis his will: Let but the commons hear this testament—Which, pardon me, I do not mean to read—And they would go and kiss dead Caesar's wounds And dip their napkins in his sacred blood..." (Act 3, Scene 2). By contrasting the thought of the citizens' revulsion at Caesar's murder with the potential benefits of his will, Antony sways public opinion.

6. **Irony**: Irony involves stating one thing while implying the opposite. Antony's entire speech is an example of verbal irony, as he keeps repeating the phrase "And Brutus is an honorable man" (Act 3, Scene 2), even while his words and tone suggest that he believes exactly the opposite.

Understanding these rhetorical devices and their use in "Julius Caesar" provides students with powerful tools for analyzing and interpreting the play, and for understanding and crafting effective communication in general.

— • —

Examples of cultural literacy

Cultural literacy refers to the ability to understand and participate fluently in a given culture. Studying Shakespeare's "Julius Caesar" contributes to cultural literacy in a variety of ways, especially as it pertains to Western culture. Here are some examples:

1. **Historical Context**: "Julius Caesar" provides insight into a crucial period in Roman history, the transition from republic to empire. Despite the dramatization, the play offers cultural literacy through understanding of historical events and figures like Caesar, Brutus, and Antony. For instance, the line "Et tu, Brute?" (Act 3, Scene 1) represents the betrayal by Brutus, one of Caesar's closest allies, which is a significant part of the historical narrative around Caesar's assassination.

2. **Understanding Shakespearean Drama**: Shakespeare's works have had a profound influence on English literature and Western culture. By studying "Julius Caesar," students gain cultural literacy about the conventions of Shakespearean tragedy, such as the tragic hero (Brutus), the tragic flaw (Brutus's idealism), and the dramatic structure (the five acts).

3. **Language and Idioms**: Many phrases that originated in Shakespeare's plays are now common idioms in English. Recognizing these idioms and understanding their context enhances cultural

literacy. For example, the phrase "Beware the Ides of March" (Act 1, Scene 2) is often used in modern language to indicate a foreboding of doom.

4. **Literary References**: Many works of literature, film, and television reference "Julius Caesar" directly or indirectly. Recognizing these references requires cultural literacy. For instance, the line "Cry 'Havoc!', and let slip the dogs of war" (Act 3, Scene 1) has been referenced in numerous modern works, from novels to movies to video games.

5. **Exploration of Universal Themes**: "Julius Caesar" explores themes such as power, loyalty, manipulation, and fate vs. free will, which are prevalent in works across cultures and eras. Understanding these themes contributes to cultural literacy. For example, Brutus's internal conflict over loyalty to Caesar vs. the good of Rome (seen throughout Act 2, Scene 1) is a universal theme that resonates in various cultural contexts.

By studying "Julius Caesar," students increase their cultural literacy, gaining a deeper understanding of Western culture and history, English literature, and universal themes.

Examples of empathy and human understanding

Shakespeare's "Julius Caesar" provides various opportunities for readers to exercise empathy and gain a deeper understanding of human nature. Here are a few examples:

1. **Brutus**: Brutus is a complex character torn between his personal loyalty to Caesar and his political commitment to Rome. Throughout the play, readers can empathize with Brutus's moral struggle. In Act 2, Scene 1, Brutus's soliloquy reveals his internal conflict, "It is not that I loved Caesar less, but that I loved Rome more." Understanding his motives and emotions can help students empathize with situations where difficult decisions have to be made.

2. **Julius Caesar**: Despite his ambition, Caesar is portrayed as a person who trusts his friends, especially Brutus. His shock and hurt at Brutus's betrayal are clear in the line "Et tu, Brute?" (Act 3, Scene 1). This gives readers a chance to empathize with Caesar, who is ultimately a victim of political conspiracy and betrayal by his closest allies.

3. **Mark Antony**: Antony's deep grief at the death of his friend and mentor, Caesar, is vividly conveyed in his soliloquy in Act 3, Scene 1: "O, pardon me, thou bleeding piece of earth, that I am meek and

gentle with these butchers!" Understanding Antony's grief and his cunning manipulation of the crowd during Caesar's funeral can offer readers insight into the complexities of human emotion and political maneuvering.

4. **The Crowd**: The easily swayed Roman populace provides an opportunity for understanding the susceptibility of crowds to persuasive rhetoric. After Brutus's speech, the crowd is ready to honor him. However, following Antony's speech, they're incensed and ready to riot against the conspirators. This can help readers empathize with and understand the vulnerability and volatility of public sentiment, particularly in charged political contexts.

In all these instances, "Julius Caesar" provides opportunities for readers to engage empathetically with the characters and their predicaments, enhancing their understanding of the complexities of human nature, including emotions, motivations, and reactions to different situations.

— · —

Examples of political philosophy and ethical dilemmas

Shakespeare's "Julius Caesar" presents numerous instances of political philosophy and ethical dilemmas. Here are some examples:

1. **Republican vs. Autocratic Rule**: The central political dilemma in "Julius Caesar" is the question of whether Rome should remain a republic, governed by the Senate, or become an empire under Caesar's rule. This issue is most evident in Brutus' and Cassius' fear of Caesar becoming a tyrant. In Act 1, Scene 2, Cassius says, "Why, man, he doth bestride the narrow world like a Colossus; and we petty men walk under his huge legs, and peep about to find ourselves dishonourable graves."

2. **Assassination for the Greater Good?**: Brutus faces a significant ethical dilemma: whether it's justified to murder Caesar, his friend, for what he perceives as the good of Rome. In Act 2, Scene 1, Brutus ponders, "And therefore think him as a serpent's egg, Which, hatched, would, as his kind, grow mischievous, And kill him in the shell." This dilemma encapsulates the concept of "the ends justify the means" in political philosophy.

3. **Manipulation of the Masses**: Both Brutus and Antony manipulate the emotions of the public for political gain, raising ethical questions about the manipulation of public sentiment for polit-

ical purposes. This is seen in Act 3, Scene 2, during the funeral speeches. Brutus appeals to the crowd's love of freedom, saying he killed Caesar to prevent their enslavement, while Antony stirs them into rebellion by highlighting Brutus' betrayal of the generous Caesar.

4. **Loyalty and Betrayal**: The theme of loyalty and its limits play a significant role in the play. Caesar's shock at Brutus's betrayal - "Et tu, Brute?" (Act 3, Scene 1) - underscores the personal pain that can arise from political actions, while Brutus's internal struggle highlights the tension between personal loyalty and the perceived good of the state.

5. **Power and Ambition**: The play also examines the corrupting influence of power and ambition. Caesar's potential ambition is the justification for his murder, while the aftermath of the assassination shows how others (like Antony and Octavius) also become consumed by their desire for power.

Through these examples, "Julius Caesar" offers a deep exploration of political philosophy and ethical dilemmas, illuminating the complexities and challenges inherent in politics and power dynamics.

Examples of public speaking and performance skills

"Julius Caesar" is filled with examples of public speaking and performance skills. The most significant instances can be seen in the funeral speeches delivered by Brutus and Mark Antony. Both characters employ different rhetorical techniques and strategies in an attempt to sway public opinion.

1. **Brutus's Speech (Act 3, Scene 2)**: Brutus employs a straight-forward, logical approach in his speech. He begins by asking the citizens to listen to his reasoning ("Hear me for my cause"), aligns himself with them by affirming their shared values ("Believe me for mine honor, and have respect to mine honor"), and then presents his argument that he loved Rome more than Caesar, and that he killed Caesar out of fear for Rome's future. Brutus also addresses the crowd as "Romans, countrymen, and lovers," demonstrating his awareness of his audience and his understanding of the need to establish a connection with them.

2. **Mark Antony's Speech (Act 3, Scene 2)**: Antony, in contrast, employs a more emotional and dramatic approach. He begins his speech by appearing to praise Brutus and the other conspirators ("But Brutus says he was ambitious; And Brutus is an honorable man") while subtly undermining their claims. Antony repeats the phrase "Brutus is an honorable man" to the point where it becomes ironic, forcing the crowd to question Brutus's actions.

Antony also appeals to the crowd's emotions by detailing Caesar's deeds for Rome and showing them Caesar's mutilated body. Additionally, Antony uses props like Caesar's will and his bloody mantle for dramatic effect.

3. **Cassius's Persuasion (Act 1, Scene 2)**: Although not a public speech, Cassius's persuasive skills can be seen when he convinces Brutus to join the conspiracy against Caesar. He appeals to Brutus's sense of honor, love for Rome, and subtly manipulates Brutus's fear of Caesar becoming a tyrant.

These scenes provide practical examples of different public speaking and persuasion techniques, such as ethos (establishing credibility), logos (use of logic and reason), pathos (appeal to emotion), the use of rhetorical questions, repetition, irony, and dramatic presentation. They can serve as useful study points for students learning about public speaking and performance skills.

— · —

Examples of understanding of dramatic devices

Shakespeare's "Julius Caesar" contains numerous dramatic devices that contribute to the play's tension, character development, and thematic exploration. Some examples include:

1. **Foreshadowing**: Shakespeare uses foreshadowing to hint at future events and create suspense. The Soothsayer's warning in Act 1, Scene 2, "Beware the ides of March," predicts Caesar's assassination. Similarly, Calpurnia's dream in Act 2, Scene 2 foreshadows Caesar's death with the image of a statue of Caesar bleeding while Romans bathe their hands in the blood.

2. **Soliloquy**: Soliloquies are speeches characters deliver when they're alone on stage, revealing their innermost thoughts and feelings. Brutus's soliloquy in Act 2, Scene 1, where he debates the conspiracy's morality, provides deep insight into his character and motivation.

3. **Irony**: Irony involves a contrast between appearance and reality. A potent instance of irony occurs when Antony repeatedly refers to Brutus as an "honorable man" in his funeral speech in Act 3, Scene 2, while implying the exact opposite, that Brutus was treacherous for betraying Caesar.

4. **Dramatic Irony**: Dramatic irony occurs when the audience

knows something that a character does not. The audience is aware of the conspiracy against Caesar, adding tension to scenes like Caesar's dismissal of the Soothsayer's warning in Act 1, Scene 2.

5. **Symbolism**: Shakespeare uses symbols to reinforce the play's themes. For example, Caesar's ghost, which appears to Brutus in Act 4, Scene 3, symbolizes Brutus's guilt and the impending doom awaiting him at Philippi.

6. **Tragic Flaw (Hamartia)**: This is a characteristic of a tragic hero that leads to their downfall. Brutus's idealism and naivety, believing that all men are as honorable as he is, can be seen as his tragic flaw leading to his downfall.

Understanding these dramatic devices enhances the appreciation and analysis of "Julius Caesar," as well as other dramatic works. It provides students with a toolkit to identify, interpret, and discuss how playwrights build compelling narratives, develop characters, and convey themes.

— · —

EXAMPLES OF CULTURAL AND HISTORICAL CONTEXT

Understanding the cultural and historical context of "Julius Caesar" can help to illuminate the themes, character motivations, and conflicts in the play. Here are some examples:

1. **Roman Republic**: "Julius Caesar" is set in 44 BC, towards the end of the Roman Republic. This period was characterized by political instability and power struggles among Rome's elite. Understanding this context can shed light on the fear Brutus and the other conspirators had about Caesar potentially becoming a tyrant. This is evident when Cassius says in Act 1, Scene 2, "Why, man, he doth bestride the narrow world like a Colossus, and we petty men walk under his huge legs and peep about to find ourselves dishonourable graves."

2. **Elizabethan England**: Shakespeare wrote "Julius Caesar" during the reign of Queen Elizabeth I. At the time, there were concerns about succession after the Queen's death as she had no heir. This may have influenced the portrayal of political power struggles in the play. Also, superstitions and omens were taken seriously in Elizabethan England, which explains the prominence of omens and supernatural elements in the play, like the Soothsayer's warning in Act 1, Scene 2, and Calpurnia's dream in Act 2, Scene 2.

3. **Classical Rhetoric**: The cultural tradition of oratory and rhetoric was highly valued in ancient Rome, and this is reflected in the eloquent speeches given by characters like Brutus and Mark Antony. Antony's funeral speech in Act 3, Scene 2, is an excellent example of classical rhetorical techniques, including ethos (establishing credibility), logos (use of logic), and pathos (appeal to emotions).

4. **Stoicism**: Stoicism was a significant philosophy in Rome, emphasizing virtue, duty, and emotional resilience. Brutus embodies these stoic values, putting his duty to Rome above his personal feelings for Caesar, as he explains in Act 2, Scene 1, "It is not that I loved Caesar less, but that I loved Rome more."

These cultural and historical contexts provide a more profound understanding of the play, the characters' motivations, and the themes Shakespeare explores.

— • —

EXAMPLES OF COMPARATIVE LITERATURE

Comparative literature involves the comparison and analysis of different works, either within one culture or across different cultures. Here are a few ways "Julius Caesar" can be compared to other texts, within the context of Shakespeare's works and more broadly:

1. **Shakespeare's Roman Plays**: "Julius Caesar" can be compared to Shakespeare's other Roman plays, "Antony and Cleopatra" and "Coriolanus." For example, all three plays explore themes of political power, loyalty, and betrayal, but they portray these themes in different ways. Brutus and Coriolanus both adhere strictly to their principles, while Antony is seen to neglect his duties for love.

2. **Tragedies of Shakespeare**: One can compare "Julius Caesar" with Shakespeare's other tragedies like "Macbeth," "Hamlet," or "King Lear." In these plays, we can find common elements such as the tragic hero with a fatal flaw (Brutus's idealism, Macbeth's ambition, Hamlet's indecisiveness, Lear's pride), the use of supernatural elements, and the exploration of themes such as power, ambition, and betrayal.

3. **Historical Writings**: The play can be compared to historical accounts of Julius Caesar's assassination, such as those found in Plutarch's "Parallel Lives." A comparative study might explore how Shakespeare dramatizes historical events, emphasizes certain

characters or themes, or deviates from historical accounts for dramatic effect.

4. **Modern Adaptations**: "Julius Caesar" can be compared to modern adaptations or reimaginings of the play or the historical events it portrays. This could involve comparing the themes, character portrayals, or the ways in which different historical periods or cultural contexts affect the interpretation of the story.

Through comparative literature, students can gain a more in-depth understanding of the themes, characters, and dramatic techniques in "Julius Caesar," as well as the ways different texts reflect their historical and cultural contexts.

— • —

EXAMPLES OF CREATIVITY

Creativity in "Julius Caesar" comes in many forms, as Shakespeare masterfully constructs a narrative that draws from history while infusing it with his own dramatic flair. Here are some examples:

1. **Inventive Use of Language**: Shakespeare's creative use of language is present throughout "Julius Caesar." He innovatively uses metaphors, similes, puns, and other forms of figurative language to enrich the dialogue and bring characters to life. For example, in Act 1, Scene 2, Cassius describes Caesar as a "Colossus" that overshadows other men, creatively using the metaphor to portray Caesar's dominance.

2. **Dramatization of Historical Events**: Shakespeare creatively reinterprets the events surrounding Julius Caesar's assassination. The historical account is filled with complex political manoeuvrings, which Shakespeare simplifies and dramatizes for the stage. For instance, in Act 3, Scene 1, Shakespeare's portrayal of Caesar's assassination is a highly dramatized spectacle, focusing on the personal betrayals and emotional impact.

3. **Characterization**: Shakespeare exercises creativity in his portrayal of historical figures. Characters like Brutus, Cassius, and Mark Antony are not merely historical figures but complex, multi-dimensional characters with unique motivations and flaws.

Brutus's internal struggle over whether to kill Caesar for the good of Rome, despite their friendship, is a particularly creative interpretation of his character.

4. **Use of Supernatural Elements**: Despite the play's historical context, Shakespeare introduces elements of the supernatural, such as omens and ghosts, to heighten the drama and foreshadow events. For example, in Act 4, Scene 3, the Ghost of Caesar appears to Brutus, symbolizing his guilt and foreshadowing his downfall.

5. **Rhetoric and Speeches**: Shakespeare's creativity is evident in the renowned speeches in the play. The funeral speeches of Brutus and Mark Antony in Act 3, Scene 2, are dramatically different and masterfully crafted, using varied rhetorical techniques to sway the citizens of Rome.

These examples illustrate how Shakespeare uses creativity to construct a compelling narrative, create complex characters, and engage audiences.

SUMMARY TO EACH ACT

Here is a detailed summary of each act in "Julius Caesar" with references:

Act 1: The play begins on February 15, 44 B.C., during the Feast of Lupercal. Caesar returns from defeating Pompey's sons in a civil war. Meanwhile, Cassius tries to persuade Brutus that Caesar is becoming too powerful and must be stopped. The Soothsayer warns Caesar to "beware the ides of March" (Act 1, Scene 2), but Caesar dismisses him. By the end of Act 1, Cassius has begun to form a conspiracy against Caesar, with Brutus considering joining.

Act 2: Brutus struggles with the decision to join the conspiracy, and after a soliloquy, he decides to join for the good of Rome (Act 2, Scene 1). The conspirators gather at Brutus's home to plan Caesar's assassination. Caesar's wife, Calpurnia, has an ominous dream of Caesar's statue bleeding while Romans bathe their hands in the blood (Act 2, Scene 2), but Decius, one of the conspirators, reinterprets the dream positively to ensure Caesar goes to the Senate.

Act 3: The conspirators carry out their plan and stab Caesar to death in the Senate. Caesar's last words to Brutus are "Et tu, Brute? Then fall, Caesar!" (Act 3, Scene 1). Brutus then addresses the public, justifying the assassination by saying that they killed Caesar out of love for Rome. Mark Antony, while seemingly supporting the conspirators, subtly turns public opinion against them in his famous speech beginning, "Friends, Romans, countrymen, lend me your ears" (Act 3, Scene 2), turning the plebeians against the conspirators.

Act 4: Antony, Octavius (Caesar's adopted heir), and Lepidus form a triumvirate to rule Rome and plan to fight against Brutus and Cassius. Brutus and Cassius have a heated argument about corruption within their ranks but reconcile when Brutus reveals that his wife, Portia, has killed herself (Act 4, Scene 3). That night, the Ghost of Caesar appears to Brutus, saying they'll meet at Philippi.

Act 5: At the Battle of Philippi, Cassius commits suicide after mistakenly believing his army has been defeated (Act 5, Scene 3). Brutus, realizing the battle is lost and unwilling to be captured, also kills himself (Act 5, Scene 5). The play concludes with Antony's speech over Brutus's body, calling Brutus the "noblest Roman of them all" (Act 5, Scene 5), as he acted out of belief for the greater good of Rome, not personal envy. The victorious Octavius agrees to give Brutus an honorable funeral.

These summaries cover the main events in each act of "Julius Caesar," highlighting the significant speeches, dramatic confrontations, and tragic moments that comprise this historical tragedy.

— · —

Summary Act i

Act 1, Scene 1: The play begins on February 15, the Feast of Lupercal, a Roman festival. Two tribunes, Flavius and Marullus, encounter a group of commoners celebrating Julius Caesar's recent victory over Pompey's sons. The tribunes scold the commoners for their fickleness, as they once celebrated Pompey's victories. They then decide to remove the decorations from Caesar's statues in an act of defiance.

    Act 1, Scene 2: Julius Caesar, accompanied by his wife Calpurnia, enters Rome to cheering crowds. A Soothsayer steps forward and cryptically warns Caesar to "Beware the ides of March" (1.2.18), but Caesar dismisses the warning. Caesar, Antony, and others depart, leaving Brutus with Cassius. Cassius begins to probe Brutus, assessing his feelings toward Caesar's growing power. Brutus admits concern but remains undecided about taking action. When Caesar returns, he confides to Antony that he's wary of Cassius, describing him as having a "lean and hungry look" (1.2.194).

    Act 1, Scene 3: Later, on a stormy night, Casca encounters Cassius. Cassius sees the storm as a sign of the gods' displeasure with Caesar's ambition. He persuades Casca to join the conspiracy he's forming against Caesar. As the scene ends, it's revealed that Brutus, though still undecided, is now considering joining the conspiracy against his friend Caesar for the good of Rome.

    This act sets up the political and personal tensions that drive the rest of the play. The stage is set for the conflict between the supporters of the

Roman Republic and those who might prefer monarchy, personified in the tension between Caesar and the growing conspiracy against him.

SUMMARY ACT 2

Act 2, Scene 1: Late into the night, Brutus ponders the conspiracy in his garden. He reflects on the necessity of killing Caesar before he can ascend to power, although Caesar has not yet done anything wrong. The other conspirators arrive, including Cassius and Casca, to finalize their plans. Brutus's wife, Portia, enters and, noticing Brutus's distressed state, begs him to confide in her. Brutus promises to reveal his troubles later.

Act 2, Scene 2: At Caesar's house, Calpurnia is deeply troubled. She has had nightmares about Caesar's death and begs him not to go to the Senate that day. Caesar initially agrees to stay home. However, Decius, one of the conspirators, arrives and reinterprets Calpurnia's dream, suggesting that it was not an omen of death but of Rome drawing new life from Caesar. Flattered, Caesar decides to go to the Senate.

Act 2, Scene 3: Artemidorus, a teacher of rhetoric who has learned about the conspiracy, reads a letter he has written to warn Caesar of the danger he is in.

Act 2, Scene 4: Portia, nervous about the plot, sends Lucius, a servant, to the Senate to see how things are proceeding and to bring back news about Caesar. The Soothsayer passes by on his way to warn Caesar, and Portia asks him to speak to Caesar and tell him to be careful.

By the end of Act 2, the plot against Caesar has been set into motion, with Brutus and the other conspirators poised to carry out their plan. Meanwhile, omens and warnings of the impending tragedy continue to surface, heightening the sense of impending doom.

—·—

Summary Act 3

Act 3, Scene 1: Caesar arrives at the Senate with the conspirators, and despite Artemidorus's attempt to present his warning letter, he does not read it. Metellus Cimber presents a petition to Caesar for his brother's banishment, and the other conspirators join in, seemingly pleading for the brother's reinstatement. When Caesar refuses, the conspirators surround him and stab him to death. Caesar's last words are "Et tu, Brute?—Then fall, Caesar" (3.1.77). The conspirators bathe their hands in Caesar's blood, and Brutus delivers a speech to the shocked onlookers, claiming that they acted for the good of Rome. Mark Antony, Caesar's loyal friend, arrives and, after assuring the conspirators of his support, asks to deliver a funeral oration for Caesar. Brutus agrees, but Cassius is suspicious.

Act 3, Scene 2: At Caesar's funeral, Brutus addresses the crowd, explaining that he loved Rome more than Caesar and that he killed Caesar out of fear of what Caesar's ambition would do to Rome. The crowd supports Brutus until Mark Antony delivers his funeral speech. Antony's speech is masterfully manipulative. He claims he has come "to bury Caesar, not to praise him" (3.2.72), but he subtly turns the crowd against the conspirators by highlighting Caesar's positive traits and questioning the justifications for the assassination. Antony then reads Caesar's will, which generously provides for the citizens of Rome, and shows them Caesar's body, causing the crowd to riot against the conspirators.

Act 3, Scene 3: The mob, in a frenzied state, encounters Cinna the poet, who shares the same name as one of the conspirators, Cinna. Despite

Cinna's pleas of mistaken identity, the mob kills him, illustrating the chaos that has engulfed Rome.

The third act of "Julius Caesar" marks the turning point of the play, with the dramatic assassination of Caesar and the equally dramatic aftermath, particularly Antony's funeral speech that sways the crowd and shifts the balance of power.

— · —

SUMMARY ACT 4

Act 4, Scene 1: Mark Antony, Octavius (Caesar's adopted heir), and Lepidus, now ruling Rome as a triumvirate, are gathered together creating a proscription list of Romans to be executed for their alleged support of the conspirators. The scene showcases the political realignment after Caesar's death and the cold pragmatism of the new rulers.

Act 4, Scene 2: Meanwhile, Brutus and Cassius have set up camp in Sardis. When Lucilius and Titinius arrive, they mention that Cassius seems to be angry with Brutus, setting the stage for a confrontation.

Act 4, Scene 3: Cassius and Brutus argue heatedly over matters of corruption and honor, highlighting their differing motivations and the strain in their relationship. Their argument is interrupted by the news of Portia's suicide, causing Brutus to reveal his deeply emotional side. Brutus and Cassius then plan their strategy for the imminent battle against Antony and Octavius. That night, Brutus is visited by the Ghost of Caesar who promises to see him again at Philippi, ominously foreshadowing the battle to come.

In this act, the unity among the conspirators starts to fray, while Antony and Octavius consolidate their power. The ghostly visitation emphasizes the weight of Brutus' decision to betray Caesar and heightens the anticipation for the final showdown at Philippi.

—•—

Summary Act 5

Act 5, Scene 1: At Philippi, the armies of Brutus and Cassius face those of Antony and Octavius. The four leaders exchange bitter words before the battle begins. Cassius and Brutus feel the weight of their decisions and acknowledge that this day might be their last.

Act 5, Scene 2: The battle begins, and Brutus sends Messala with orders to Cassius' forces.

Act 5, Scene 3: As the battle unfolds, Cassius believes that his side is losing because of a misinterpretation of a signal. Overwhelmed by what he perceives as defeat, he asks his servant Pindarus to help him commit suicide, believing that he'd rather die than be captured.

Act 5, Scene 4: Brutus, however, is still fighting vigorously and urges his soldiers to continue. He learns of Cassius's death and mourns the loss of his friend.

Act 5, Scene 5: As the battle continues, Brutus, isolated and desperate, also chooses suicide rather than capture. He runs onto his own sword held by his servant Strato. Antony, finding Brutus' body, respects his enemy by calling him the "noblest Roman of them all" (5.5.68), noting that Brutus was the only conspirator who acted for what he genuinely believed was the good of Rome. Octavius, now the unchallenged leader of Rome, offers to give Brutus a noble funeral, ending the play on a note of respect for the fallen Brutus.

Act 5 encapsulates the tragic climax and resolution of the play. The fates of Brutus and Cassius underscore the personal tragedies that unfold in parallel with Rome's political upheaval. Their suicides signal the end of the old Roman Republic, and Octavius's final victory sets the stage for the rise of the Roman Empire.

— • —

Main characters

Here are the main characters in William Shakespeare's "Julius Caesar":

1. **Julius Caesar**: Despite the play being named after him, Caesar is not the protagonist but an important catalyst in the plot. He is the powerful Roman political leader who is assassinated by conspirators who fear that his ambition will lead to tyranny.

2. **Marcus Brutus**: Often considered the tragic hero of the play, Brutus is a respected Roman senator who joins the conspiracy against Caesar out of concern for the Roman Republic. His internal struggle between personal loyalty and public duty forms a significant element of the tragedy.

3. **Cassius**: Cassius is the instigator of the conspiracy against Caesar. He is politically savvy, manipulative, and leads other senators, including Brutus, into the conspiracy out of envy and fear of Caesar's rising power.

4. **Mark Antony**: Antony is Caesar's loyal friend and right-hand man who, after Caesar's death, incites the people of Rome against the conspirators with his stirring funeral speech. Antony's actions lead to a civil war against the conspirators.

5. **Octavius Caesar**: Octavius is Julius Caesar's adopted heir. He is a relatively minor character until the end of the play, where he

assumes power alongside Antony following the defeat of Brutus and Cassius.

6. **Portia**: Portia is Brutus's wife and the daughter of a Roman nobleman. She is concerned for her husband, and her suicide is one of the play's tragic moments.

7. **Calpurnia**: Julius Caesar's wife, who has prophetic dreams about her husband's murder and attempts to prevent him from going to the Senate on the Ides of March.

8. **Casca**: One of the conspirators against Caesar, Casca is a cynical and frightened man who is easily manipulated by Cassius.

Each of these characters plays a crucial role in the dramatic events of the play and contributes to its exploration of power, loyalty, ambition, and honor.

JULIUS CAESAR

Julius Caesar is a central character of Shakespeare's play, although his time on stage is relatively short compared to other major characters. He is a powerful leader of Rome who has just returned from defeating Pompey's sons in battle.

Caesar is presented as being greatly admired and perhaps also feared. The common people of Rome adore him and celebrate his victories, as shown in Act 1, Scene 1. However, among the Roman senators, there is concern that his increasing popularity and ambition may threaten the Roman Republic.

Shakespeare's depiction of Caesar is complex. While Caesar is certainly ambitious, as shown in his disregard for the Soothsayer's warning to "Beware the ides of March" (Act 1, Scene 2), he also exhibits the qualities of a good leader. He appears generous, as demonstrated in his will, where he leaves a portion of his wealth and property to the people of Rome (Act 3, Scene 2), and confident, as seen in his refusal to change his decision in response to Artemidorus' letter (Act 3, Scene 1).

Yet, Caesar is not entirely without flaws. He is dismissive of his wife Calpurnia's fears for his safety (Act 2, Scene 2), showing a certain arrogance or overconfidence. He also dismisses the Soothsayer's warning, indicating a potential ignorance or dismissive attitude toward omens and portents.

Caesar's most significant moment, of course, comes with his death. When Brutus, a man he considered a friend, joins the conspirators in assassinating him, Caesar's final words are, "Et tu, Brute? Then fall, Caesar!"

(Act 3, Scene 1). This famous line conveys a sense of betrayal and surprise that Brutus would join the conspiracy against him.

Despite his death in Act 3, Caesar's influence and presence persist throughout the play, with his ghost appearing to Brutus (Act 4, Scene 3), and his name being invoked by both the conspirators and Antony as they vie for control of Rome.

Overall, Shakespeare's Caesar is a compelling figure whose ambition, authority, and eventual assassination catalyze the events of the play and whose influence extends far beyond his life.

— · —

Caesar's positive characteristics

The title character is portrayed with several positive qualities that contribute to his high status and popularity in Rome.

1. **Leadership**: Caesar is a strong leader who has just returned from successfully defeating the sons of his rival Pompey, an event that opens the play. His leadership skills are evident in his military successes and his command over the people of Rome.

2. **Generosity**: Despite accusations of ambition, Caesar is shown to be generous. In his will, revealed by Mark Antony in Act 3, Scene 2, Caesar leaves his personal gardens to the public and a sum of money to every Roman citizen.

3. **Confidence**: Caesar displays confidence and courage, refusing to hide from potential threats. For instance, he dismisses the Soothsayer's warning to "Beware the ides of March" (Act 1, Scene 2) and decides to attend the Senate despite Calpurnia's ominous dreams (Act 2, Scene 2).

4. **Resoluteness**: Caesar shows firmness in his decisions, demonstrating his strong will and conviction. An example is when he refuses to pardon Metellus Cimber's banished brother in Act 3, Scene 1, indicating that he is not a leader who can be easily swayed.

5. **Dignity**: Even in death, Caesar retains his dignity. His last words,

"Et tu, Brute? Then fall, Caesar!" (Act 3, Scene 1), show a powerful acceptance of his fate once he sees his friend Brutus among the assassins.

6. **Influence**: Caesar's influence extends beyond his life. His memory becomes a significant political tool that Mark Antony uses against the conspirators, and his ghost haunts Brutus, indicating his lasting impact.

These positive traits, combined with his flaws, make Caesar a complex and compelling character in Shakespeare's play.

CAESAR'S NEGATIVE CHARCTERISTICS

In "Julius Caesar," Shakespeare presents the title character as a complex figure with several perceived negative traits. These traits contribute to the growing fear and resentment among the conspirators, which ultimately leads to his assassination.

1. **Ambition**: Caesar is often portrayed as overly ambitious, which stirs the fear that he seeks absolute power and will establish a monarchy, thus undermining the Roman Republic. This trait is most explicitly mentioned by Brutus in Act 2, Scene 1: "The lowliness is young ambition's ladder, / Whereto the climber upward turns his face; / But when he once attains the upmost round, / He then unto the ladder turns his back."

2. **Arrogance**: Caesar can also come across as arrogant or overconfident. This is demonstrated when he dismisses the Soothsayer's warning to "Beware the ides of March" in Act 1, Scene 2, and his refusal to heed his wife Calpurnia's dream premonitions in Act 2, Scene 2.

3. **Inflexibility**: While Caesar's firmness in his decisions can be viewed as a strength, it can also be seen as a negative trait. His refusal to revoke the banishment of Metellus Cimber's brother in Act 3, Scene 1, despite pleas from other senators, shows a lack of mercy or flexibility.

4. **Dismissiveness**: Caesar dismisses the concerns and fears of those close to him. For example, he ignores his wife Calpurnia's pleas not to go to the Senate on the Ides of March (Act 2, Scene 2), suggesting a certain level of disregard for the feelings and opinions of others.

5. **Ignorance towards omens**: Caesar tends to ignore or underestimate omens and supernatural signs, which can be seen as a flaw. Besides ignoring the Soothsayer's warning, he also ignores Calpurnia's disturbing dream, which foretells his death.

These characteristics, when viewed from the perspective of the conspirators, justify their concerns that Caesar's rule could lead to the downfall of the Roman Republic. In this way, these traits contribute to the tragic events of the play.

— · —

WHAT LED TO CAESAR'S DOWNFALL

Julius Caesar's downfall in Shakespeare's play is a result of a combination of factors, which ultimately lead to his assassination on the Ides of March (March 15th).

1. **Ambition**: Caesar's ambition to rise to power and become a monarch is perceived as a threat to the Roman Republic by the conspirators. His ambition is seen by others, particularly Brutus and Cassius, as a dangerous quality that could lead to tyranny.

2. **Arrogance and Overconfidence**: Caesar's arrogance is another key contributor to his downfall. He dismisses the Soothsayer's warning to "Beware the Ides of March" (Act 1, Scene 2) and ignores his wife Calpurnia's prophetic dream about his murder (Act 2, Scene 2). His overconfidence in his own invulnerability blinds him to the impending threat.

3. **Disregard for Omens and Prophecies**: Despite numerous omens and prophecies forewarning Caesar of his assassination, he chooses to ignore them, attributing them to fear and cowardice. His dismissal of these warnings directly leads him into the hands of his murderers.

4. **Betrayal**: Perhaps the most significant factor leading to Caesar's downfall is the betrayal by his close friend Brutus, whom Caesar trusts and respects. When Brutus joins the conspirators, it not

only increases their credibility but also leads to a successful plot against Caesar. When Caesar sees Brutus among his assassins, he delivers the famous line, "Et tu, Brute? Then fall, Caesar!" (Act 3, Scene 1). The shock and betrayal in this moment epitomize Caesar's downfall.

5. **Public Opinion**: Caesar's popularity among the Roman people proves to be a double-edged sword. While it helps him rise to power, it also fosters resentment among the senators and fear that he may become a tyrant.

Caesar's downfall, though tragic, serves as a central event in the play, setting off a chain of events that lead to a civil war and ultimately the end of the Roman Republic.

— · —

CAESAR'S INFLUENCE AFTER HIS DEATH

Julius Caesar's influence persists long after his death and shapes the rest of the events in Shakespeare's play. Here are a few key ways in which his influence is felt:

1. **Mark Antony's Speech**: Caesar's death sets the stage for one of the most famous speeches in literature: Mark Antony's funeral oration. Antony uses his speech to manipulate public opinion, turning the Roman citizens against the conspirators by pointing out Caesar's love for Rome, his generosity (demonstrated in his will), and questioning the accusation of ambition that Brutus used to justify the murder. In this way, Caesar's memory becomes a powerful political tool.

2. **Civil War**: The aftermath of Caesar's assassination leads to a power struggle that eventually turns into a civil war. The alliance between Antony, Octavius (Caesar's adopted heir), and Lepidus, collectively known as the Second Triumvirate, directly results from Caesar's death. They fight against the forces of Brutus and Cassius, leading to further bloodshed.

3. **Brutus' Torment**: Brutus, who considered Caesar a friend, is haunted by guilt and remorse after Caesar's assassination. He is literally haunted by Caesar's ghost in Act 4, Scene 3, symbolizing his inner torment and the continuing influence of Caesar.

4. **Octavius' Rise**: Caesar's death allows Octavius, his adopted son and heir, to rise to power. After defeating Brutus and Cassius, Octavius becomes one of the three men who control the Roman Empire, fulfilling Caesar's legacy.

5. **Continuation of Caesar's Policies**: In historical terms, Caesar's policies continued under the reign of Octavius (later known as Augustus), which helped to shape the future of the Roman Empire.

Thus, even after his death, Julius Caesar remains a powerful force in the play, shaping the events and the destinies of the remaining characters. The transformation of the Roman Republic into the Roman Empire, which is not depicted in the play but is the historical aftermath of Caesar's death, can also be seen as a testament to his enduring influence.

Marcus Brutus

Marcus Brutus is one of the main characters in Shakespeare's "Julius Caesar" and is the tragic hero of the play. He is a senator and a close friend of Caesar, but his loyalty to Rome and his fear of Caesar's ambition lead him to become a key conspirator in the plot to assassinate Caesar.

1. **Noble and Honorable**: Brutus is portrayed as noble and deeply honorable. He believes in the value of the Roman Republic and is committed to its preservation. This is evident when he says in Act 2, Scene 1, "Not that I loved Caesar less, but that I loved Rome more," explaining his reasoning for joining the conspiracy against Caesar.

2. **Patriotic**: Brutus' patriotism is a significant characteristic. He is driven by a sense of duty to Rome rather than personal ambition or resentment. This is what sets him apart from the other conspirators, particularly Cassius, who is driven by envy and personal resentment against Caesar.

3. **Idealistic**: Brutus is idealistic, often to the point of being naive. He believes that all the conspirators are as honorable as he is and share his high-minded motives, a belief that Antony takes advantage of in his funeral speech in Act 3, Scene 2.

4. **Inner Conflict**: Brutus is a character marked by inner conflict. He struggles greatly with his decision to kill Caesar, as shown

in Act 2, Scene 1, where he wrestles with his conscience and his loyalty to his friend Caesar versus his perceived duty to Rome. This inner turmoil is a key element of his character throughout the play.

5. **Manipulable**: Despite his nobility, Brutus is somewhat easily manipulated. This is most evident in Act 1, Scene 2, when Cassius flatters and persuades Brutus that Caesar must be killed for the good of Rome. Brutus' acceptance of Cassius's manipulative arguments leads to his tragic downfall.

6. **Remorse and Guilt**: After Caesar's assassination, Brutus is wracked with guilt and remorse. This is seen in Act 4, Scene 3, when the ghost of Caesar appears, symbolizing Brutus's guilt and the ongoing influence of Caesar in the aftermath of his death.

7. **Tragic Hero**: Brutus fits the archetype of a tragic hero. He is a man of high standing who is led by a tragic flaw (his idealism and naivety) to make decisions that lead to tragedy (Caesar's assassination and subsequent civil war) and his own downfall (his suicide in Act 5).

Throughout the play, Brutus' actions, driven by his noble and patriotic but also idealistic nature, have significant consequences, making him one of the most important and complex characters in "Julius Caesar".

CASSIUS

Cassius is a central character in Shakespeare's "Julius Caesar." He is a senator of Rome and the instigator of the conspiracy against Caesar. Here are some key characteristics of Cassius as portrayed in the play:

1. **Envious and Resentful**: Cassius is often portrayed as being envious of Caesar's power and position. In Act 1, Scene 2, he says to Brutus, "I was born free as Caesar; so were you: / We both have fed as well, and we can both / Endure the winter's cold as well as he."

2. **Manipulative and Persuasive**: Cassius is highly manipulative, particularly in his interactions with Brutus. He convinces Brutus to join the conspiracy against Caesar by playing on his fears and love for the Roman Republic. For example, in Act 1, Scene 2, Cassius tells Brutus that "the fault, dear Brutus, is not in our stars, / But in ourselves, that we are underlings."

3. **Strategic and Cunning**: Cassius demonstrates his strategic and cunning nature when he forges letters from the Roman citizens to convince Brutus of Caesar's threat to the Republic. His strategy is revealed in Act 1, Scene 2: "I will this night, / In several hands, in at his windows throw, / As if they came from several citizens."

4. **Pragmatic and Realistic**: Unlike Brutus, Cassius is more pragmatic and less idealistic. He objects to allowing Antony to speak

at Caesar's funeral (Act 3, Scene 1) because he understands the potential for Antony to sway public opinion, demonstrating a more realistic view of human nature and politics.

5. **Paranoid and Superstitious**: Unlike Caesar, Cassius is very superstitious and believes strongly in omens. In Act 5, Scene 1, he says, "I know these omens will be followed by the wrath of the gods," showing his fear and belief in the supernatural.

6. **Determined**: Cassius is highly determined in his mission to kill Caesar, which demonstrates his strong will. He is so committed to the cause that he is willing to die if Caesar becomes king, as expressed in Act 1, Scene 2: "I know where I will wear this dagger then; / Cassius from bondage will deliver Cassius."

Throughout the play, Cassius acts as a foil to Brutus, highlighting Brutus' idealism and honor with his own pragmatism and manipulation. His machinations are central to the plot of the play and have a lasting impact on the events that follow Caesar's assassination.

Mark Antony

Mark Antony is one of the central characters in William Shakespeare's "Julius Caesar." He starts as a loyal friend to Caesar and transforms into a skilled politician and an avenger following Caesar's assassination.

1. **Loyal**: Antony's loyalty to Caesar is one of his defining traits. He is depicted as a close friend to Caesar and is consistently loyal to him. This loyalty extends even after Caesar's death, as he seeks to avenge his friend. His loyalty is evident when he asks to be killed along with Caesar in Act 3, Scene 1: "O, pardon me, thou bleeding piece of earth, / That I am meek and gentle with these butchers! / Thou art the ruins of the noblest man / That ever lived in the tide of times."

2. **Skilled Orator**: One of Antony's most notable traits is his ability as a speaker, which he demonstrates in his funeral speech for Caesar in Act 3, Scene 2. He skillfully uses rhetoric to stir the crowd against the conspirators, turning public opinion against them: "Friends, Romans, countrymen, lend me your ears; / I come to bury Caesar, not to praise him."

3. **Manipulative**: Antony shows his manipulative side when he uses Caesar's will and his own speech at Caesar's funeral to incite the crowd against the conspirators. His manipulation is seen when he says, in Act 3, Scene 2, "But here's a parchment with the seal

of Caesar; / I found it in his closet, 'tis his will: / Let but the commons hear this testament / (Which, pardon me, I do not mean to read)..."

4. **Political Acumen**: Antony exhibits political acumen in his alliance with Octavius and Lepidus to form the Second Triumvirate. He skillfully maneuvers to eliminate his political enemies and consolidate power, showing his strategic thinking and political savvy.

5. **Ambitious**: Antony shows his ambition when he seizes power after Caesar's death and consolidates his rule through the Triumvirate. His ambition is further seen in his eagerness to divide the Roman territories with Octavius and Lepidus in Act 4, Scene 1.

6. **Vengeful**: After Caesar's death, Antony seeks to avenge his fallen friend. His desire for revenge drives him to incite the mob against the conspirators and wage war against Brutus and Cassius.

Through Antony's character, Shakespeare explores themes of loyalty, manipulation, power, and the dynamics of political leadership. Antony's transformation from a loyal friend to a ruthless politician contributes to the tragic events that unfold following Caesar's assassination.

Octavius Caesar

Octavius Caesar, later known as Augustus Caesar in history, is a significant character in Shakespeare's "Julius Caesar". He is the adopted son and heir of Julius Caesar and forms part of the Second Triumvirate along with Antony and Lepidus following Caesar's assassination.

1. **Youthful yet Commanding**: Octavius is introduced in the play as a young man, but despite his youth, he asserts his authority. He insists on taking the right flank in the battle against Brutus and Cassius despite Antony's suggestion to the contrary. This occurs in Act 5, Scene 1: "I do not cross you; but I will do so."

2. **Determined and Unyielding**: Octavius demonstrates determination and a refusal to yield to others, even those who are his seniors or supposedly his allies. This can be seen in his interaction with Antony where he sticks to his decision against Antony's advice, revealing his strong will.

3. **Strategist**: Octavius shows his strategic prowess in the play. After the death of Caesar, he forms the Second Triumvirate with Antony and Lepidus to consolidate power and avenge Caesar's death. His political maneuvering indicates his strategic thinking and leadership capabilities.

4. **Just**: Octavius is depicted as being fair-minded and just. When Antony suggests killing relatives who may pose a threat, Octavius

disagrees, saying in Act 4, Scene 1: "And some that smile have in their hearts, I fear, / Millions of mischiefs."

5. **Legacy of Julius Caesar**: As Julius Caesar's adopted son and heir, Octavius carries forward the legacy of Julius Caesar. He steps into Caesar's shoes after his death and effectively continues Caesar's influence over Rome and its empire.

6. **Victorious**: In the end, it's Octavius who emerges victorious in the civil war that follows Caesar's assassination, hinting at his future role as the first emperor of Rome, Augustus Caesar.

Octavius' character in the play, though not as extensively developed as some of the others, represents the future of Rome and serves as a glimpse of the historical figure of Augustus Caesar, who established the Roman Empire following the events of the play.

PORTIA

Portia is a notable character in Shakespeare's "Julius Caesar." She is Brutus' wife and the daughter of a Roman nobleman, Cato. Although her presence in the play is brief, she provides a significant perspective and emotional depth to the story.

1. **Loyal and Devoted**: Portia is depicted as a loyal and devoted wife to Brutus. Despite his preoccupation with the conspiracy against Caesar, she remains supportive and understanding. Her loyalty and concern for Brutus are evident in Act 2, Scene 1: "Within the bond of marriage, tell me, Brutus, / Is it excepted I should know no secrets / That appertain to you?"

2. **Intelligent and Perceptive**: Portia is intelligent and highly perceptive. She notices Brutus' internal struggle even when he attempts to hide it, suggesting her deep understanding and intuition. In Act 2, Scene 1, she says to Brutus, "You've ungently, Brutus, / Stole from my bed: and yesternight, at supper, / You suddenly arose, and walked about, / Musing and sighing..."

3. **Courageous**: Portia shows her bravery when she wounds herself in the thigh to prove her strength and loyalty to Brutus, as shown in Act 2, Scene 1: "I have made strong proof of my constancy, / Giving myself a voluntary wound / Here, in the thigh..."

4. **Emotional Depth**: Portia is one of the few female characters in

the play, and her emotions add depth to the narrative. Her worry for Brutus and her anxiety over the conspiracy bring a humanizing element to the story.

5. **Tragic End**: The news of Portia's suicide in Act 4, Scene 3, which she undertakes out of despair and anxiety following Brutus's departure from Rome, adds to the overall tragedy of the play.

In the context of "Julius Caesar," Portia serves as a symbol of the personal cost of the political events in the play. Her loyalty, perception, and tragic fate underscore the human elements of the story amidst the political plotting and intrigue.

CALPURNIA

Calpurnia is a lesser of the main characters, yet an impactful character in William Shakespeare's "Julius Caesar." She is the wife of Julius Caesar and is primarily remembered for her attempt to dissuade Caesar from going to the Senate on the Ides of March due to her prophetic dream of his death.

1. **Prophetic**: Calpurnia has a prophetic dream that foreshadows Caesar's death, demonstrating a certain connection to the supernatural. In Act 2, Scene 2, she describes her dream to Caesar, saying, "I have seen tonight / Methought I saw you [Caesar] scaled with bleeding wounds / Many good Romans come to you and weep."

2. **Persuasive**: Calpurnia is persuasive when trying to convince Caesar to stay home from the Senate due to her ominous premonitions. In Act 2, Scene 2, she insists, "Do not go forth today: call it my fear / That keeps you in the house, and not your own."

3. **Caring and Protective**: Her attempts to keep Caesar at home demonstrate her protective nature and deep care for her husband. She is deeply concerned for his safety, as seen in Act 2, Scene 2: "Alas, my lord, / Your wisdom is consumed in confidence. / Do not go forth today."

4. **Superstitious**: Like many Romans, Calpurnia believes in omens and dreams, and her dream and interpretation thereof reflect this

belief. In Act 2, Scene 2, she implores Caesar, "The heavens themselves blaze forth the death of princes."

Despite her limited appearance in the play, Calpurnia's role is significant. Her prophetic dream and attempts to persuade Caesar not to attend the Senate on the Ides of March emphasize the dramatic tension and impending doom that lead to Caesar's assassination. Her concern for Caesar's safety adds an emotional layer to the unfolding political events

CASCA

Casca is one of the conspirators against Julius Caesar in William Shakespeare's "Julius Caesar." His character, while not as developed as others like Brutus or Antony, serves a pivotal role in the plot of the play.

1. **Plain-speaking and Cynical**: Casca is known for his plain, blunt speech and cynical view of the world. He is often sarcastic, as seen in Act 1, Scene 2, when he describes to Brutus and Cassius how Caesar refused the crown offered to him by Antony: "I saw Mark Antony offer him a crown (yet 'twas not a crown neither, 'twas one of these coronets) and, as I told you, he put it by once—but, for all that, to my thinking, he would fain have had it."

2. **First to Strike**: Casca is the first to stab Caesar during the assassination in Act 3, Scene 1, marking a critical point in the play's plot development. The moment is punctuated by his line: "Speak, hands, for me!"

3. **Persuadable**: Casca is shown to be easily swayed by others, particularly Cassius, who manipulates him into joining the conspiracy against Caesar. Cassius plays on Casca's fear of Caesar becoming a tyrant to involve him in the plot.

4. **Superstitious**: Casca is noticeably superstitious, which is highlighted during the storm in Act 1, Scene 3. He views the storm and other unusual phenomena as omens indicating that something

terrible will happen in Rome: "Are not you moved, when all the sway of earth / Shakes like a thing unfirm?"

Casca's character contributes to the sense of impending doom and the chaotic environment that leads to Caesar's assassination. His actions and views add to the exploration of themes such as manipulation, power, and fear within the play.

— · —

MINOR CHARCTERS

"Julius Caesar" by William Shakespeare has numerous minor characters that contribute to the richness and complexity of the plot, even though they don't have as significant roles as characters like Caesar, Brutus, Antony, or Cassius. Here are some of these minor characters:

1. **Cicero**: A Roman senator who speaks at the festival of Lupercalia, Cicero is wise and respected, but he is not included in the conspirators' plans because they believe he will not follow any plan started by someone else.

2. **Murellus and Flavius**: These are two tribunes (officials) who disapprove of the adoration of the masses for Caesar. They are responsible for removing decorations from Caesar's statues during Caesar's triumphal parade.

3. **Decius Brutus**: Not to be confused with the main character Brutus (Marcus Brutus), Decius is one of the conspirators against Caesar. He is responsible for persuading Caesar to attend the Senate on the Ides of March despite Calpurnia's warnings.

4. **Metellus Cimber**: A conspirator who draws Caesar's attention by requesting his banished brother's pardon, thereby creating a diversion for the conspirators to carry out their plan.

5. **Trebonius**: Another conspirator, Trebonius lures Antony away

from the Senate House so that he cannot help Caesar during the assassination.

6. **Cinna the Poet**: He is mistaken for Cinna the conspirator and killed by the angry mob after Mark Antony's incendiary speech, highlighting the chaos and confusion in Rome.

7. **Lucilius, Titinius, and Messala**: Friends and allies of Brutus and Cassius, they play key roles in the events leading to the battles of Philippi.

8. **Soothsayer**: An important minor character who warns Caesar to "Beware the Ides of March."

9. **Artemidorus**: He tries to warn Caesar of the conspiracy by presenting him a letter, but Caesar does not read it.

These characters, despite their minor roles, significantly contribute to the events and the overall progression of the plot in "Julius Caesar."

WHAT ARE THE IMPORTANT RELATIONSHIPS

Several relationships in Shakespeare's "Julius Caesar" are integral to the play's development, conflict, and resolution. Here are some of them:

1. **Julius Caesar and Brutus**: Brutus is torn between his personal affection for Caesar and his political ideals of preserving the Roman Republic. Caesar trusts Brutus and is genuinely shocked when Brutus stabs him, saying the famous line, "Et tu, Brute? Then fall, Caesar." (Act 3, Scene 1).

2. **Brutus and Cassius**: The friendship and political alliance between Brutus and Cassius form the heart of the conspiracy against Caesar. Their relationship has its ups and downs, including a notable argument in Act 4, Scene 3, but they ultimately unite against a common enemy. Their contrasting personalities (Brutus' idealism versus Cassius' pragmatism) create tension but also a dynamic synergy.

3. **Brutus and Portia**: Portia, as Brutus's wife, is one of the few characters who can penetrate Brutus's stoic exterior. She's worried about him and insists on knowing what's troubling him in Act 2, Scene 1. Brutus's reaction to the news of Portia's death in Act 4, Scene 3, underscores the depth of their relationship.

4. **Julius Caesar and Calpurnia**: Caesar's relationship with Calpurnia provides insight into his personal life. Despite his im-

age as a fearless leader, he respects his wife's fears and concerns about the omens she has seen, until Decius reinterprets Calpurnia's dream and convinces Caesar to go to the Senate in Act 2, Scene 2.

5. **Mark Antony and Caesar**: Antony is loyal to Caesar and passionately avenges his death. His relationship with Caesar gives him a motive for stirring up rebellion in Rome with his funeral speech (Act 3, Scene 2) and aligning with Octavius to defeat Brutus and Cassius.

6. **Mark Antony and Octavius**: Initially, there seems to be tension between Antony and Octavius, as seen in their disagreements in Act 4. However, they unite in their mission to avenge Caesar's death and gain control over Rome, demonstrating a strategic political alliance.

7. **The Conspirators**: The relationship between the group of conspirators is fraught with tension and mistrust. They share a common goal of removing Caesar, but their motives and methods vary, leading to a disjointed and ultimately unsuccessful rebellion.

Each of these relationships serves to highlight the themes of loyalty, betrayal, honor, and power that pervade the play.

Details about Caesar and Brutus' relationship

The relationship between Julius Caesar and Brutus in Shakespeare's "Julius Caesar" is one of the key dynamics in the play, filled with personal affection, political conflict, and ultimately, betrayal.

1. **Personal Affection**: The personal affection between Caesar and Brutus is evident. Brutus is well-regarded by Caesar, and there is a deep bond of friendship and trust between them. Caesar's famous last words, "Et tu, Brute?—Then fall, Caesar!" (Act 3, Scene 1), highlight the depth of his surprise and hurt at Brutus's participation in the assassination. This line also underscores the personal, rather than merely political, nature of Brutus's betrayal.

2. **Political Conflict**: Despite this affection, Brutus finds himself torn between his love for Caesar and his love for Rome. He fears that Caesar's ambition will lead to tyranny and the end of the Roman Republic. This political conflict is articulated in Act 2, Scene 1, when Brutus says, "It must be by his death: and for my part, / I know no personal cause to spurn at him, / But for the general."

3. **Ultimate Betrayal**: The climax of their relationship comes in the Senate House on the Ides of March. Despite his deep respect and affection for Caesar, Brutus becomes one of his assassins. His

personal conflict between his love for his friend and his perceived duty to Rome is evident when he says, "Not that I loved Caesar less, but that I loved Rome more" (Act 3, Scene 2).

4. **Caesar's High Regard for Brutus**: Despite Brutus joining the conspirators, Caesar's high regard for Brutus never wanes. In Act 2, Scene 2, Caesar dismisses his wife Calpurnia's fears about the omens of his death, asserting his faith in Brutus: "We have the falling sickness. I have no fear, / For the heart of Brutus yearns to think upon."

This complex relationship between Caesar and Brutus adds to the dramatic tension and tragic nature of the play, encapsulating themes of friendship, duty, betrayal, and the personal cost of political actions.

Details about Brutus and Cassius' relationship

The relationship between Brutus and Cassius forms a significant subplot of Shakespeare's "Julius Caesar". Their alliance, based on a shared political ideal, contains moments of disagreement, tension, and mutual respect. Here are some key aspects of their relationship:

1. **Formation of Alliance**: Cassius initiates the alliance by persuading Brutus to join the conspiracy against Caesar. In Act 1, Scene 2, Cassius uses flattery and manipulative rhetoric to kindle Brutus's fear of Caesar's ambition: "Why should that name be sounded more than yours? / Write them together, yours is as fair a name...".

2. **Differences in Motives**: Brutus is portrayed as an honorable Roman driven by his desire to uphold the Roman Republic's ideals. He explains his decision to join the conspiracy in Act 2, Scene 1: "Not that I loved Caesar less, but that I loved Rome more." On the other hand, Cassius's motivations seem more personally driven, rooted in jealousy and resentment towards Caesar's rising power.

3. **Differences in Strategy**: In Act 4, Scene 3, Brutus and Cassius have a major argument about military strategy. Brutus advocates for meeting Antony and Octavius's forces at Philippi, while Cassius advises against it. This disagreement exposes their contrasting personalities—Brutus's idealistic and somewhat naive approach

versus Cassius's pragmatic and cautious strategy.

4. **Reconciliation and Mutual Respect**: Despite their differences, Brutus and Cassius reconcile after their argument, demonstrating mutual respect and the strength of their friendship. After learning of Portia's death, Cassius shows genuine sympathy for Brutus: "I am sorry that by hanging her / You have lost the immortal part of her / And with her, the mortal part." (Act 4, Scene 3).

5. **Shared Tragedy**: Ultimately, both Brutus and Cassius meet tragic ends, further binding their stories together. In their final moments, they each acknowledge their guilt and regret over the assassination of Caesar, adding a poignant layer to their friendship.

Through the complex relationship between Brutus and Cassius, Shakespeare explores themes such as friendship, manipulation, honor, and the personal implications of political decisions.

— • —

DETAILS ABOUT BRUTUS AND PORTIA'S RELATIONSHIP

Brutus and Portia share a relationship characterized by mutual respect, affection, and trust, despite the political turmoil unfolding around them. Here are some details about their relationship:

1. **Portia's Concern for Brutus**: In Act 2, Scene 1, Portia shows her deep concern for Brutus, who has been acting strangely due to his involvement in the conspiracy against Caesar. She pleads with him to confide in her: "I should not know you, Brutus. / Dear my lord, / Make me acquainted with your cause of grief."

2. **Brutus' Affection and Respect for Portia**: Brutus clearly loves and respects his wife, acknowledging her strength and courage. He reveals his affection when he refers to her as "my dear, dear Portia" (Act 2, Scene 1).

3. **Portia's Persuasiveness**: Portia is able to persuade Brutus to reveal his secrets to her, displaying her understanding of her husband and her ability to convince him. She argues that as the daughter of Cato and the wife of Brutus, she is strong enough to carry the burden of his concerns: "Tell me your counsels, I will not disclose 'em: / I have made strong proof of my constancy" (Act 2, Scene 1).

4. **Portia's Distress and Suicide**: After Brutus leaves Rome, Portia

is filled with anxiety and fear. In Act 4, Scene 3, Brutus is informed of Portia's suicide, and his reaction reveals his deep love and sorrow for her loss: "Speak no more of her. Give me a bowl of wine. / In this I bury all unkindness, Cassius" (Act 4, Scene 3).

5. **Brutus' Regret**: After learning of Portia's death, Brutus is filled with regret, suggesting that he understands the cost of his decisions and the pain they've caused those he loves.

Portia's character is important not only as Brutus's wife but also as one of the few female characters in the play. Her strength, wisdom, and loyalty serve to highlight the personal, emotional implications of the political chaos that unfolds.

Details about Julius Caesar and Calpurnia's relationship

The relationship between Julius Caesar and his wife Calpurnia in Shakespeare's "Julius Caesar" provides an important look into Caesar's private life and offers insight into his personality outside of the political sphere.

1. **Caesar's Regard for Calpurnia**: Despite his image as a strong, authoritative leader, Caesar shows that he takes Calpurnia's concerns seriously. This is evident when she warns him of the omens of his death in Act 2, Scene 2. Initially, Caesar decides to heed her advice and stay home: "Mark Antony shall say I am not well, / And, for thy humor, I will stay at home."

2. **Calpurnia's Protective Instinct**: Calpurnia's care for Caesar is evident in her fearful reaction to her prophetic dream about his assassination. She pleads with him to stay home for his safety in Act 2, Scene 2: "Do not go forth today: call it my fear / That keeps you in the house, and not your own."

3. **Caesar's Decision to Leave**: Caesar's decision to leave the house after all, persuaded by Decius's reinterpretation of Calpurnia's dream, reveals his susceptibility to flattery and his desire to appear fearless. This decision, despite Calpurnia's pleas, foreshadows his downfall.

4. **Calpurnia's Intuition**: Calpurnia's dream of Caesar's statue

spouting blood, and her desperate attempts to keep him home, demonstrate her intuition and insight into the impending danger, creating dramatic irony since the audience is aware of the plot against Caesar.

Overall, the relationship between Caesar and Calpurnia underscores the theme of fate versus free will and the tragic consequences of ignoring warnings. It also gives a more personal dimension to Caesar's character, showcasing his respect for his wife's opinion and his own superstitious nature.

Details about Mark Antony and Caesar's relationship

In "Julius Caesar", Shakespeare presents Mark Antony and Julius Caesar as close allies with a relationship characterized by mutual respect and loyalty. Here are some key details about their relationship:

1. **Antony's Loyalty to Caesar**: Antony's deep loyalty to Caesar is evident throughout the play. In Act 1, Scene 2, Antony shows his devotion by offering to touch Calpurnia during the race in the Feast of Lupercal, as part of a ritual to cure her infertility, at Caesar's request. This act signifies Antony's respect and obedience towards Caesar.

2. **Caesar's Trust in Antony**: Caesar trusts Antony implicitly and sees him as a loyal friend. In Act 1, Scene 2, Caesar confides in Antony about his suspicion of Cassius, indicating his trust in Antony's discretion and loyalty.

3. **Antony's Grief and Call for Revenge**: Antony's reaction to Caesar's death underscores his loyalty and affection for Caesar. In Act 3, Scene 1, he expresses his grief at Caesar's death and his intent for revenge: "O, pardon me, thou bleeding piece of earth, / That I am meek and gentle with these butchers! / Thou art the ruins of the noblest man / That ever lived in the tide of times."

4. **Antony's Manipulation of the Crowd**: In Act 3, Scene 2,

Antony delivers a powerful speech at Caesar's funeral that incites the crowd against the conspirators. This speech reveals Antony's cunning and his determination to avenge Caesar's death. He manipulates the crowd by repeatedly calling the conspirators "honourable men" while demonstrating the effects of their brutal act.

5. **Antony's Dedication to Upholding Caesar's Legacy**: In the later acts of the play, Antony's actions are driven by his dedication to uphold Caesar's legacy. He forms the Second Triumvirate with Octavius and Lepidus to seize control of Rome and to counter the forces of Brutus and Cassius.

The relationship between Antony and Caesar serves as a key component in the play's progression. Antony's loyalty to Caesar sets the stage for his transformation from a seemingly hedonistic supporter of Caesar to a cunning and capable political leader after Caesar's assassination.

Details about Mark Antony and Octavius' relationship

In "Julius Caesar," Shakespeare portrays the relationship between Mark Antony and Octavius Caesar as complex and sometimes contentious, balancing on their shared objective of avenging Caesar's death and maintaining control over Rome. Below are key points of their relationship:

1. **Shared Power and Common Goal**: After Julius Caesar's assassination, Mark Antony and Octavius form the Second Triumvirate along with Lepidus to seize control of Rome and avenge Caesar's death. This represents their shared power and a common goal (Act 4, Scene 1).

2. **Tension and Disagreement**: Despite their alliance, Antony and Octavius often disagree, indicating tension within their relationship. A clear example is their disagreement over whether to engage Brutus and Cassius at Philippi. Antony, the more experienced soldier, argues that they should wait and let their enemies come to them, but Octavius insists on moving to Philippi (Act 4, Scene 3). This shows a difference in their approach and a budding power struggle.

3. **Disparagement of Lepidus**: Antony also expresses contempt for Lepidus, their Triumvirate colleague, calling him a mere "property" and a "slight unmeritable man" (Act 4, Scene 1). This exposes

Antony's domineering side, and although Octavius defends Lepidus, it's another source of friction between them.

4. **Battle against Brutus and Cassius**: Together, Antony and Octavius successfully defeat Brutus and Cassius in the Battle of Philippi, which leads to both Brutus's and Cassius's suicides. Their alliance holds, even as they differ on military strategy, showcasing their united front against the common enemy.

5. **Mutual Respect**: Despite their differences, Antony and Octavius show a level of mutual respect. After Brutus's death, Antony eulogizes Brutus, calling him the "noblest Roman of them all" (Act 5, Scene 5), and Octavius agrees, displaying their capacity to put aside their own ambition and recognize the merits of their adversary.

Antony and Octavius's relationship in the play foreshadows the historical events that occurred after Julius Caesar's death: the power struggle between them leading to the final war of the Roman Republic, with Octavius (later known as Augustus) ultimately becoming the first Roman Emperor.

— • —

WHAT ARE THE THEMES

"Julius Caesar" by William Shakespeare tackles numerous themes with complexity. These themes are explored through the characters' actions and dialogues. Here are some of the themes with references from the play:

1. **Ambition and Power**: The theme of ambition and power is most evident through the character of Julius Caesar, who's feared to become too powerful by the senators. In Act 1, Scene 2, Cassius says to Brutus, "Why, man, he [Caesar] doth bestride the narrow world / Like a Colossus; and we petty men / Walk under his huge legs, and peep about / To find ourselves dishonorable graves."

2. **Manipulation and Rhetoric**: The power of rhetoric and manipulation is explicitly illustrated in Antony's funeral speech for Caesar in Act 3, Scene 2. He skillfully uses pathos and rhetorical devices to manipulate the crowd against the conspirators: "Friends, Romans, countrymen, lend me your ears; / I come to bury Caesar, not to praise him."

3. **Fate vs. Free Will**: The theme of fate versus free will is clearly shown when Caesar ignores the Soothsayer's warning. Despite the Soothsayer's famous warning in Act 1, Scene 2 — "Beware the ides of March" — Caesar eventually chooses to ignore these prophetic words, leading to his death.

4. **Friendship and Betrayal**: Brutus's internal conflict about be-

traying his friend Caesar for the greater good of Rome illustrates the theme of friendship and betrayal. In Act 2, Scene 1, Brutus reflects, "It must be by his death: and for my part, / I know no personal cause to spurn at him, / But for the general."

5. **Honor and Duty**: Brutus embodies the theme of honor and duty. He believes that his participation in Caesar's assassination is for the betterment of Rome, as he says in Act 3, Scene 2: "Not that I loved Caesar less, but that I loved / Rome more."

6. **Public vs. Private Life**: Caesar's disregard of Calpurnia's dream in Act 2, Scene 2, choosing instead to maintain his public image, underscores the tension between public duty and private concerns: "Cowards die many times before their deaths; / The valiant never taste of death but once."

7. **Mortality and Legacy**: Caesar's influence beyond his death illustrates the theme of mortality and legacy. In Act 3, Scene 2, Antony predicts the civil unrest following Caesar's death, showing how Caesar's legacy continues to impact Rome: "And Caesar's spirit, ranging for revenge, / With Ate by his side come hot from hell, / Shall in these confines with a monarch's voice / Cry 'Havoc!' and let slip the dogs of war."

By exploring these themes, Shakespeare provides a timeless study of power dynamics, human nature, and ethical dilemmas.

Describe ambition and power theme

The theme of ambition and power is central to William Shakespeare's "Julius Caesar." This theme is primarily explored through the characters of Caesar, Brutus, and Cassius, and their various interactions and motivations.

1. **Julius Caesar**: Despite being a successful leader and widely loved by the public, Caesar's ambition for power seems boundless, and this raises concerns among the senators. In Act 1, Scene 2, Cassius tells Brutus, "Why, man, he [Caesar] doth bestride the narrow world / Like a Colossus, and we petty men / Walk under his huge legs and peep about / To find ourselves dishonourable graves." This metaphor illustrates Caesar's enormous power and influence, with the other men dwarfed beneath him.

2. **Brutus and Cassius**: Brutus and Cassius, key conspirators against Caesar, are motivated by their own ambitions for power, albeit presented differently. Cassius harbors an explicit resentment towards Caesar's growing power and is driven by a desire to assert his own influence. In Act 1, Scene 2, he says to Brutus, "I was born free as Caesar; so were you: / We both have fed as well, and we can both / Endure the winter's cold as well as he." Cassius asserts his equality with Caesar, challenging the superiority of Caesar's power.

Brutus, on the other hand, portrays his ambition as driven by a sense of duty and honor for Rome, rather than personal gain. Yet, his decision to join the conspiracy demonstrates his desire to control Rome's destiny. In Act 2, Scene 1, he says, "It must be by his death: and for my part, / I know no personal cause to spurn at him, / But for the general." Here, Brutus declares that killing Caesar is a necessity, driven by his perceived duty to Rome rather than personal animosity.

3. **Mark Antony**: After Caesar's death, Antony's ambition becomes more apparent. He skillfully manipulates the public sentiment to turn against the conspirators and aligns with Octavius to defeat Brutus and Cassius, thus securing power for himself. In Act 3, Scene 2, Antony, during his funeral oration, carefully manipulates the crowd, "You all did love him once, not without cause: / What cause withholds you then, to mourn for him?" Here, Antony's cunning rhetoric turns the people of Rome against the conspirators, leading to a shift in power.

In conclusion, the theme of ambition and power underpins the motivations of various characters in "Julius Caesar," driving the narrative forward and shaping the tragic events of the play.

— • —

Describe manipulation and rhetoric theme

The theme of manipulation and rhetoric is crucial to "Julius Caesar." William Shakespeare masterfully demonstrates how language can be used as a powerful tool for persuasion and manipulation.

1. **Cassius Manipulating Brutus**: One of the first major instances of manipulation occurs when Cassius begins to persuade Brutus to join the conspiracy against Caesar. Cassius understands Brutus's honorable nature and uses this to his advantage. He manipulates Brutus's love for Rome to convince him that Caesar must be stopped for the good of the republic. In Act 1, Scene 2, Cassius states, "The fault, dear Brutus, is not in our stars, / But in ourselves, that we are underlings." Here, Cassius cleverly places the responsibility of Rome's downfall on Brutus's inaction, playing on his honor and love for Rome.

2. **Brutus's Speech at Caesar's Funeral**: After Caesar's assassination, Brutus uses rhetoric to justify his actions to the Roman people. In Act 3, Scene 2, he begins his speech by addressing the Romans as "Romans, countrymen, and lovers," emphasizing their shared nationality and his own camaraderie with them. He repeatedly asserts that he loved Caesar but loved Rome more, thus framing his act as one borne out of necessity rather than personal gain: "Not that I loved Caesar less, but that I loved / Rome more." This explanation successfully convinces the crowd momentarily.

3. **Antony's Funeral Oration**: Antony's speech at Caesar's funeral is one of the most famous examples of rhetorical skill in literature. Antony uses rhetorical questions, repetition, and irony to provoke the crowd's emotions and incite them against the conspirators. His repeated statement, "But Brutus says he was ambitious; / And Brutus is an honourable man," becomes increasingly ironic as he reveals the deeds that contradict Caesar's alleged ambition. The crowd is effectively swayed by Antony's manipulation of their feelings, leading to a riot.

4. **Decius Convincing Caesar**: In Act 2, Scene 2, Caesar initially decides to stay home due to the ominous signs and his wife Calpurnia's dream. However, Decius manages to reinterpret Calpurnia's dream favorably and diminishes the significance of the omens, convincing Caesar to go to the Senate. This demonstrates how manipulation can have fatal consequences.

In each of these examples, characters use rhetoric and manipulation to further their ambitions, demonstrating the power of language to shape events. The theme of manipulation and rhetoric is thus intricately woven into the play, driving the narrative forward.

DESCRIBE FATE VS. FREE WILL THEME

The theme of fate versus free will is a significant and thought-provoking aspect of "Julius Caesar." Shakespeare grapples with these philosophical concepts throughout the play, as characters navigate between their perceived destinies and their individual choices.

1. **Ignoring Omens**: Julius Caesar's life is riddled with omens and prophecies, which he largely chooses to ignore. This is particularly evident when he disregards the Soothsayer's warning. In Act 1, Scene 2, the Soothsayer warns Caesar to "Beware the ides of March," a prophetic cautioning of his forthcoming death. Despite the explicit warning, Caesar chooses to ignore it, demonstrating his belief in his own free will over predetermined fate.

2. **Caesar's Hubris**: Even when confronted with multiple omens, such as his wife Calpurnia's dream of his statue spouting blood (Act 2, Scene 2), Caesar still insists on going to the Senate on the Ides of March. He says, "Cowards die many times before their deaths; / The valiant never taste of death but once." These lines reflect Caesar's belief that he can overcome fate through bravery and willpower.

3. **Brutus's Decision**: Brutus's decision to join the conspiracy against Caesar is also a significant moment that reflects this theme. He battles with the dilemma of whether to allow Rome's fate to

unfold under Caesar's rule or to intervene by exercising his own free will. In Act 2, Scene 1, he ponders, "The fault, dear Brutus, is not in our stars, / But in ourselves, that we are underlings." Brutus concludes that it's up to them to act against Caesar, asserting human agency over predestined fate.

4. **The Ghost of Caesar**: In Act 4, Scene 3, Brutus is visited by the Ghost of Caesar, which prophesizes Brutus's defeat at Philippi. Despite this apparition, Brutus chooses to confront Antony and Octavius in battle, highlighting once more the struggle between fate and free will.

In each of these instances, Shakespeare explores how the characters grapple with their perceived destiny and the power of their own choices, creating a complex interplay between fate and free will. This theme contributes significantly to the depth and tragic essence of the play.

DESCRIBE FRIENDSHIP AND BETRAYAL THEME

The themes of friendship and betrayal in "Julius Caesar" are closely interwoven and are key drivers of the plot. This duality creates a tragic tension within the characters and the overall narrative.

1. **Brutus and Caesar**: Brutus and Caesar share a close friendship, and it's implied that Caesar sees Brutus almost like a son. Yet Brutus betrays Caesar for what he perceives as the greater good of Rome. When Caesar sees Brutus among his assassins, he utters the famous line in Act 3, Scene 1, "Et tu, Brute?—Then fall, Caesar." This phrase encapsulates the magnitude of Brutus's betrayal, emphasizing the deep personal connection between the two men.

2. **Brutus and Cassius**: Brutus and Cassius also share a complex friendship. Cassius manipulates Brutus into joining the conspiracy against Caesar, exploiting Brutus's honor and patriotism. In Act 1, Scene 2, Cassius says, "I will this night, / In several hands, in at his windows throw, / As if they came from several citizens, / Writings all tending to the great opinion / That Rome holds of his name." Here, Cassius sets up his plan to sway Brutus through deceit, a form of betrayal within their friendship. Despite this, Brutus and Cassius share several genuine moments of friendship throughout the play, particularly in Act 4, Scene 3, when they reconcile after a heated argument.

3. **Antony, Octavius, and Lepidus**: Following Caesar's assassination, Antony, Octavius, and Lepidus form a political alliance to combat the conspirators. However, the friendship between the three is tenuous and fraught with power struggles. Antony expresses his dismissive opinion about Lepidus in Act 4, Scene 1, stating "This is a slight unmeritable man, / Meet to be sent on errands." This lack of trust and mutual respect hints at the potential for betrayal within their alliance.

In all these relationships, Shakespeare explores the themes of friendship and betrayal, showing how they can coexist and contribute to the tragic downfall of the characters. These themes underpin the complexity of human relationships and the moral dilemmas faced by individuals when torn between personal affections and political obligations.

Describe honor and duty theme

The theme of honor and duty in "Julius Caesar" is predominantly seen through the character of Brutus. As an honorable man torn between his loyalty to Caesar and his duty to Rome, Brutus personifies this conflict, which is central to the play's tragic tension.

1. **Brutus's Inner Conflict**: Brutus's struggle to reconcile his duty to Rome with his friendship with Caesar is a major aspect of his character. In Act 2, Scene 1, Brutus muses, "It must be by his death: and for my part, / I know no personal cause to spurn at him, / But for the general." Here, Brutus reasons that, for the greater good of Rome, Caesar must die, despite Brutus's personal affection for him. This shows the weight he places on his perceived duty above personal relationships.

2. **Brutus's Honor**: Brutus's sense of honor is frequently referenced throughout the play, even by his enemies. Antony, after Brutus's death in Act 5, Scene 5, declares, "This was the noblest Roman of them all: / All the conspirators save only he / Did that they did in envy of great Caesar; / He only, in a general honest thought / And common good to all, made one of them." This reflects that, despite his role in the assassination of Caesar, Brutus's motivation was rooted in his sense of honor and duty, not personal ambition or malice.

3. **The Role of Duty in Conflict**: The sense of duty also extends to the battlefield. Both sides of the conflict—Brutus and Cassius versus Antony and Octavius—believe they fight for the betterment of Rome. This mutual yet opposing sense of duty fuels the conflict and ultimately leads to a tragic end for many of the characters.

4. **The Final Actions of Brutus**: In the end, Brutus chooses to commit suicide, viewing it as a final honorable act rather than being captured by the enemy. In Act 5, Scene 5, Brutus says, "I shall have glory by this losing day / More than Octavius and Mark Antony / By this vile conquest shall attain unto." He views his death as a noble sacrifice, a testament to his enduring sense of duty and honor.

The theme of honor and duty thus underscores the tragic dilemmas faced by characters, particularly Brutus, and shapes the dramatic events of "Julius Caesar." It offers an exploration of the tension between personal loyalty and public responsibility.

— • —

DESCRIBE PUBLIC VS. PRIVATE LIFE THEME

The conflict between public and private life is a significant theme in "Julius Caesar". It showcases the tension between characters' personal desires, beliefs, and relationships, and their public roles and responsibilities.

1. **Julius Caesar**: Caesar's character embodies this struggle. He is aware of the public perception of him as an ambitious and potential dictator, but he also grapples with his own vulnerabilities and superstitions in his private life. For example, in Act 2, Scene 2, despite presenting a front of bravery to the public, he confides in his wife Calpurnia about the various omens and her unsettling dream. However, Decius convinces him to disregard his private fears for the sake of public appearance, leading to his assassination.

2. **Brutus**: Brutus, too, struggles to reconcile his private affection for Caesar with his public duty to Rome. In Act 2, Scene 1, he wrestles with his decision in a soliloquy: "It must be by his death: and for my part, / I know no personal cause to spurn at him, / But for the general." This shows how Brutus sets aside his private feelings in favor of his public responsibility.

3. **Antony**: Antony, while a loyal friend to Caesar, also understands the importance of public perception. After Caesar's death, he hides his true feelings to negotiate with the conspirators in public, but privately mourns Caesar's death and vows revenge (Act 3,

Scene 1). Later, he skillfully manipulates the public sentiment with his funeral speech, despite his private grief.

4. **Portia and Calpurnia**: Both Portia (Brutus's wife) and Calpurnia (Caesar's wife) suffer due to their husbands' public lives. Despite their private concerns and insights, their influence is limited. For example, in Act 2, Scene 2, Calpurnia's plea for Caesar to stay home is overridden by Decius's manipulation.

In all these instances, the tension between public duties and private emotions adds depth to the characters and drives the plot. It emphasizes the tragic cost of political life and highlights the personal struggles beneath public personas.

— · —

DESCRIBE MORTALITY AND LEGACY THEME

The themes of mortality and legacy are central to "Julius Caesar." Shakespeare explores these themes in the context of political power, friendship, and ambition, highlighting the characters' aspirations for immortality and the often unforeseen consequences of their actions.

1. **Caesar's Mortality and Legacy**: Despite his position of power and the almost god-like reverence some characters show for him, Caesar is not invincible. His mortality is cruelly demonstrated in his assassination in Act 3, Scene 1. However, Caesar's influence does not end with his death. His legacy becomes a powerful symbol in the hands of Mark Antony, used to manipulate the populace and wage a war against the conspirators. His will, as read by Antony in Act 3, Scene 2, demonstrates his posthumous generosity towards the people of Rome, further inflaming the public against his murderers.

2. **Brutus and Legacy**: Brutus, too, is acutely aware of the legacy he wants to leave behind. He joins the conspiracy against Caesar, believing that it's for the greater good of Rome. His primary concern is the preservation of the republic and its freedom, which he believes will be his enduring legacy. Yet, after his death in Act 5, Scene 5, Mark Antony describes Brutus as "the noblest Roman of them all," recognizing that his intentions were pure compared to the other conspirators. This unexpected acknowledgment forms

part of Brutus's legacy.

3. **Antony and Octavius's Legacy**: Antony and Octavius, in avenging Caesar's death and taking control of Rome, are also mindful of their legacy. They are conscious of how they would be remembered and make strategic decisions, such as their manipulation of Caesar's will and legacy, to ensure their place in Roman history.

4. **Cassius and Legacy**: Cassius, who instigates the conspiracy, also contemplates his legacy, albeit in a different way. He is motivated primarily by envy and personal ambition, with little concern for the welfare of Rome. His legacy, therefore, is largely negative, even in his own eyes, as evidenced by his suicide in Act 5, Scene 3.

In summary, "Julius Caesar" deeply explores the themes of mortality and legacy. While all characters face inevitable death, their legacies are determined by their actions, motivations, and how they are perceived by others. This creates a dramatic interplay between the characters' immediate decisions and their far-reaching impacts.

CONFLICTS

"Julius Caesar" is rife with conflict, both external and internal. Here are some key conflicts in the play:

1. **Political Conflict**: The most evident conflict in the play is the political struggle for power in Rome. Caesar's increasing influence and ambition alarm a group of senators, leading to a conspiracy against him. Cassius incites this conflict in Act 1, Scene 2 when he says to Brutus, "Why, man, he doth bestride the narrow world / Like a Colossus, and we petty men / Walk under his huge legs and peep about / To find ourselves dishonourable graves."

2. **Internal Conflict within Brutus**: Brutus grapples with a significant internal conflict between his love for Caesar and his love for Rome. In Act 2, Scene 1, Brutus deliberates in a soliloquy, "It must be by his death: and for my part, / I know no personal cause to spurn at him, / But for the general," signaling his decision to put Rome's interests over his friendship with Caesar.

3. **Rhetorical Conflict**: There's a major rhetorical conflict in Act 3, Scene 2 during the funeral speeches. Brutus seeks to justify Caesar's assassination to the Roman citizens, arguing it was necessary for Rome's freedom. Antony, however, subtly counters Brutus's arguments, provoking the crowd into rebellion against the conspirators.

4. **Conflict between Conspirators**: Tension and conflict arise within the group of conspirators themselves. In Act 4, Scene 3, Brutus and Cassius argue over military strategy and Cassius's alleged corruption, revealing their differing motivations and approaches.

5. **Battle Conflict**: The climax of the play is a physical battle at Philippi between the forces of Antony and Octavius (Caesar's avengers) and those of Brutus and Cassius (the conspirators), as depicted in Act 5.

6. **Conflict between Public and Private Selves**: Many characters experience conflict between their public duties and their private feelings. A key example is when Caesar dismisses his personal concerns about the omens and his wife Calpurnia's pleas to stay home to maintain his public image (Act 2, Scene 2).

These conflicts drive the plot of "Julius Caesar," leading to its tragic conclusion. They underscore the play's themes of ambition, honor, betrayal, and the tension between public and private life.

DESCRIBE THE POLITICAL CONFLICT

The political conflict in "Julius Caesar" primarily centers around the question of who should hold power in Rome and the nature of that power. The entire narrative is driven by the tension that emerges from these disagreements.

1. **Threat of Dictatorship**: The first glimpse of the political conflict is seen in the fear of Julius Caesar becoming a dictator. Despite Caesar's popularity with the common people, some senators perceive his ambition as a threat to the Roman Republic. Cassius articulates this fear to Brutus in Act 1, Scene 2: "Why, man, he doth bestride the narrow world / Like a Colossus, and we petty men / Walk under his huge legs and peep about / To find ourselves dishonourable graves."

2. **Conspiracy and Assassination**: The political conflict escalates with the conspiracy to assassinate Caesar. The senators, particularly Brutus and Cassius, believe they are acting in the best interest of Rome. Brutus argues this in his soliloquy in Act 2, Scene 1: "And for my part, / I know no personal cause to spurn at him, / But for the general. He would be crown'd: / How that might change his nature, there's the question."

3. **Aftermath of Assassination**: Following Caesar's assassination, the political conflict does not end but intensifies. Mark Antony, a

loyal friend of Caesar, skillfully turns the Roman populace against the conspirators with his famous funeral speech in Act 3, Scene 2: "Friends, Romans, countrymen, lend me your ears; / I come to bury Caesar, not to praise him."

4. **Civil War**: The political conflict culminates in a civil war. Antony, allied with Octavius, fights against Brutus and Cassius's forces to avenge Caesar's death and seize control of Rome. This conflict is depicted in Act 5, with the Battle of Philippi marking the climax of the political struggle.

The political conflict in "Julius Caesar" ultimately leads to a shift in Rome's power structure, with the Republic giving way to an Empire under Octavius. This progression demonstrates the unpredictable and often violent nature of political power struggles.

Describe internal conflict within Brutus

Brutus's internal conflict is one of the central elements of "Julius Caesar". His struggle lies in his personal affection for Caesar and his sense of duty to Rome. His love for Caesar competes with his love for Roman republicanism, creating a moral dilemma that he must navigate throughout the play.

1. **Love for Caesar vs. Duty to Rome**: This internal conflict is introduced in Act 1, Scene 2, when Cassius plants the seeds of doubt in Brutus's mind about Caesar's ambition. Brutus cares for Caesar but also fears the potential threat he poses to the Republic. This is reflected in his lines: "What means this shouting? I do fear the people / Choose Caesar for their king... yet I love him well."

2. **Decision to Join the Conspiracy**: The conflict within Brutus deepens when he contemplates joining the conspiracy against Caesar. In Act 2, Scene 1, Brutus delivers a soliloquy that provides a glimpse into his internal struggle: "It must be by his death: and for my part, / I know no personal cause to spurn at him, / But for the general." This shows that Brutus, despite having no personal grievances against Caesar, feels compelled to act for the general good of Rome.

3. **Aftermath of the Assassination**: Following Caesar's assassination, Brutus continues to grapple with his decision. During his

speech in Act 3, Scene 2, Brutus attempts to justify his actions to himself and the crowd: "If then that friend demand why Brutus rose against Caesar, this is my answer: Not that I loved Caesar less, but that I loved Rome more."

4. **Conflict with Cassius**: Brutus's internal conflict also manifests in his disagreements with Cassius, as seen in Act 4, Scene 3. While Cassius is driven by envy and self-interest, Brutus is guided by a sense of duty and honor, leading to heated arguments and adding another layer to Brutus's internal struggle.

5. **Brutus's Death**: Brutus's internal conflict concludes with his death in Act 5, Scene 5. Accepting responsibility for his actions, Brutus states, "I killed not thee with half so good a will," acknowledging that his noble intentions have resulted in tragic outcomes.

In all, Brutus's internal conflict adds a layer of complexity to "Julius Caesar," illustrating the moral ambiguities of political decisions and highlighting the personal costs of public actions.

Describe rhetorical conflict

Rhetoric plays a pivotal role in "Julius Caesar," particularly in the persuasive speeches that contribute to the political and emotional tensions throughout the play. The most significant instance of rhetorical conflict occurs in Act 3, Scene 2, during the funeral speeches given by Brutus and Mark Antony.

1. **Brutus' Speech**: After the assassination of Julius Caesar, Brutus seeks to justify their actions to the crowd. His approach is rational, calm, and appeals to the audience's sense of Roman virtue. He uses the rhetoric of patriotism, arguing that Caesar's ambition threatened the freedom of all Romans: "Not that I loved Caesar less, but that I loved Rome more" (Act 3, Scene 2). By framing the assassination as an act of patriotism, Brutus tries to win the public's approval.

2. **Mark Antony's Speech**: Antony's speech, which follows Brutus', is a masterclass in rhetorical manipulation. Although he begins by seemingly endorsing Brutus' points ("I come to bury Caesar, not to praise him"), Antony gradually undermines the conspirators' arguments, using repetition, irony, and emotional appeal. He repeatedly refers to the conspirators as "honorable men" while highlighting Caesar's achievements and kindness, effectively turning the crowd against them.

3. **The Power of Rhetoric**: The crowd's shift from supporting Brutus to revolting against the conspirators illustrates the power of rhetoric. Antony's speech, while emotionally charged and seemingly less rational than Brutus', ultimately proves more effective. The phrase "And Brutus is an honorable man" (Act 3, Scene 2) evolves from an endorsement to a biting piece of irony that highlights the conspirators' deceit.

4. **Conflict Result**: This rhetorical conflict leads to real, tangible conflict. The crowd is moved by Antony's words and incites a riot, leading to a civil war against Brutus and the conspirators, showing that words can be as potent as swords.

In "Julius Caesar," the rhetorical conflict is not merely a battle of words but a driving force behind the play's events. The differing rhetorical strategies and their consequences showcase the power and danger of persuasive speech.

DESCRIBE THE CLIMAX OF THE PLAY

The climax of Shakespeare's "Julius Caesar" is arguably the Battle of Philippi, particularly the events of Act 5, Scene 3, where both Cassius and Titinius meet their tragic ends, followed by Brutus's realization of their deaths and his own impending defeat.

1. **Cassius's Misinterpretation and Suicide**: Cassius sends Titinius to check on the status of his forces and, from a distance, misinterprets what he sees, thinking that Titinius has been captured by enemy troops. Overcome by guilt and despair, Cassius chooses to end his life, instructing Pindarus to help him: "Guide thou the sword—Pindarus, I that denied / Thee to my bosom, do thee with this requital. / Be satisfied, my good Pindarus, for I / Have here received letters that young Octavius / And Mark Antony come down upon us with / A mighty power, bending their expedition / Toward Philippi." (Act 5, Scene 3)

2. **Titinius's Suicide**: Titinius returns after Cassius's suicide to announce that their side was actually winning the battle. Discovering Cassius's body and realizing his misinterpretation, Titinius also kills himself out of grief, marking another tragic event in the climax.

3. **Brutus's Realization**: Brutus discovers the bodies of Cassius and Titinius, and he begins to understand that his cause is lost. His line

"O Julius Caesar, thou art mighty yet! / Thy spirit walks abroad, and turns our swords / In our own proper entrails." (Act 5, Scene 3) indicates his realization of Caesar's posthumous influence and the magnitude of his own impending defeat.

Although the play continues for two more scenes, the events of Act 5, Scene 3 mark the climax or turning point of the story because it is at this point that the ultimate fate of the main characters is effectively sealed. Brutus's forces are defeated, leading to his suicide in Act 5, Scene 5, and Antony and Octavius eventually consolidate power, marking the end of the Roman Republic.

DESCRIBE THE RESOLUTION OF THE PLAY

The resolution of "Julius Caesar" takes place in Act 5, Scene 5, with the deaths of Brutus and the consequent end of the civil war.

1. **Brutus's Suicide**: Recognizing that his army is defeated and unwilling to be captured and paraded through Rome in humiliation, Brutus decides to kill himself. He runs onto his own sword, held by his servant Strato. As he dies, Brutus says, "Caesar, now be still. / I killed not thee with half so good a will" (Act 5, Scene 5). This statement reveals Brutus's final recognition that his noble intentions led to disastrous outcomes, including the loss of his own life.

2. **Mark Antony's Eulogy**: After Brutus's death, Mark Antony delivers a final speech, acknowledging Brutus as the only conspirator who acted for the good of Rome rather than out of envy of Caesar. Antony says, "This was the noblest Roman of them all...His life was gentle, and the elements / So mix'd in him that Nature might stand up / And say to all the world 'This was a man!'" (Act 5, Scene 5). These words show Antony's respect for Brutus, despite their political differences.

3. **Octavius's Ascendance**: The play concludes with Octavius taking control of Rome, symbolizing the end of the Roman Republic and the beginning of the Roman Empire. He says, "So call the

field to rest, and let's away / To part the glories of this happy day" (Act 5, Scene 5). These words indicate Octavius's victory and his readiness to establish his rule.

The resolution of the play brings closure to the political and personal conflicts that have driven the plot, but it also underscores the tragic cost of these conflicts, the transition from a republic to an empire, and the enduring complexities of ambition, power, loyalty, and honor.

WHAT IS THE MORAL OF THE STORY

"Julius Caesar" is a complex play with various themes and interpretations, so different readers may take away different morals from the story. However, a few key lessons can be distilled from the plot and character arcs:

1. **The Perils of Ambition**: Caesar's ambition, which leads him to ignore warnings about his impending doom, proves to be his downfall. Similarly, Brutus's ambition to safeguard the Republic leads him to participate in a brutal assassination. Thus, unchecked ambition can lead to ruin, no matter how noble the intention.

2. **The Consequences of Betrayal**: Brutus's betrayal of his friend Caesar not only fails to preserve the Republic but also leads to civil war, death, and his own suicide. Betrayal, even when committed for what seems like the right reasons, has severe consequences.

3. **The Power of Rhetoric**: Mark Antony's manipulation of public sentiment through rhetoric leads to a violent uprising, illustrating the power of words and their potential to incite action.

4. **The Complexity of Moral Choices**: Brutus's dilemma over killing Caesar illustrates that moral choices are rarely clear-cut and can lead to unexpected and tragic outcomes.

5. **The Uncertainty of Fate**: Despite the many prophecies and omens in the play, the characters struggle to interpret these signs

correctly, suggesting that it's challenging to predict or control one's fate.

6. **Public vs. Personal Life**: The play shows the tension between public duty and personal loyalty, as seen in Brutus's conflict between his duty to Rome and his loyalty to Caesar.

These morals provide a cautionary tale about power, ambition, betrayal, and the complexities of moral decision-making, all of which remain relevant today.